MOOD

INTERIORS & INSPIRATION BY
ANNE HEPFER

EDITED BY BETH HITCHCOCK
PRINCIPAL PHOTOGRAPHY BY VIRGINIA MACDONALD

GIBBS SMITH
TO ENRICH AND INSPIRE HUMANKIND

DEDICATION

For Christian, my best friend and my love.
Your loving support and incomparable enthusiasm for life is the best gift,
and one you continue to give me and the kids every day.
Thank you from the bottom of my heart.

To Jack, Charlie, Amelia, and Alexander:
Keep shining bright. I am very proud and humbled to be your mom.
Love you to the moon and back.

SEPTEMBER 2011

CONTE

NTS

5

6

7

n empty room is a canvas—a place to play with composition and contrast, scale and proportion. Using both my training and my instincts, I call on muses as diverse as the countries I've visited, artisans I've admired, and songs I've sung around a campfire. For me, "home" is not only an aesthetic. It's a feeling.

We live in a stressed-out, fast-paced world and time is our most precious commodity. When I'm not with family and friends, I feel grateful to spend my time building spaces where my clients can escape, cocoon, and recharge. To create a meaningful home, we must examine how we want to feel in our private spaces and how we interact with them morning, noon and night; those decisions can set the tone for each day. Our moods live deep within us—the ultimate expression of ourselves—and are triggered by memories, dreams, scents, and experiences home and abroad, alone or shared with loved ones.

If you've ever experienced a craving, you know food conjures moods as well—that's why I've included a handful of crowd-pleasing dishes my family and friends love to share when we sit down for quality time together. And almost nothing lifts us up or mellows us out like music, so I've created mood-specific playlists and sprinkled them throughout. As you listen to the melodies and lyrics, I hope you'll experience deep moments of discovery and déjà vu.

As much as I revel in time spent at home, I long to get out and explore. "Wanderlust" is my favorite word and my deep, ongoing desire to travel and learn is a big part of who I am and what I do. When I travel, I treasure hunt—not only for beautiful works from local makers but for the colors, forms, and cultural wisdom that leave an impression on my brain and heart, and find a way into the spaces I design.

I'm on the lookout for painters, basket weavers, ceramicists, rug makers, textile printers—you name it. By the time I pack to return home, my suitcase and carry-on are usually bursting with beautifully designed pieces to add to my own home or share with my clients.

That's why this book is more than just a collection of my beloved interior design projects—it's a passport. Come along on this journey through the people, places, and things that motivate and move me. I hope to spark your imagination, and help you turn your home into a bold canvas that reflects your many moods and fills your rooms with laughter, music, and beauty.

GETTING TO KNOW YOU

When I begin a new project, I ask my clients to complete an extensive questionnaire. It's an icebreaker, and a meaningful tool that helps me get to know what inspires and excites them. It seems only fair to turn the tables and try a version of it myself before we embark on this journey together.

 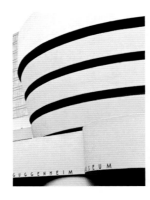  

Favorite Things

PIECE OF FURNITURE
Womb Chair by Eero Saarinen. I have a pair in my office, and I admire them every day—the perfect combination of comfort and sculpture.

ART
Monet's Water Lilies. The first time I visited the Musée de l'Orangerie I was awestruck by Monet's giant, overscaled paintings. I felt as if I were swimming among the waterlilies, surrounded by mesmerizing changing color palettes.

FASHION DESIGNER
Brunello Cuccinelli. His attention to fine detail is truly inspiring, not to mention the depth of neutrals and layers of textures in his designs. The flip side of me loves **Tory Burch** for her play on patterns, vibrant use of colors, and her savvy translation of global textiles into current ready-to-wear.

COLOR
British racing car green. Super sexy. Need I say more?

SCENT
Neroli Portofino by Tom Ford. Makes me feel like I'm zipping around the winding curves of the Amalfi Coast in a vintage MG convertible.

BOOK
Beloved by Toni Morrison. I first encountered this book during my African American studies course at Vanderbilt. It deeply moved me and has stuck with me through the years.

Getaway Goals

HOTEL CHAIN
Oberoi in India for their impeccable service, and, of course, beautiful rooms filled with luxurious colors, patterns, tassels, and contrast trimmings.

NEXT DESTINATION
Japan, to walk through the iconic temples, shrines, streets, and markets; to shop for textiles, ceramics, and objects; to taste the variety of foods; to see and smell the cherry blossoms.

BEACH
St. Barths in the winter, where you can dine with your feet in the sand overlooking the turquoise sea. **Nantucket** in the summer, where we love to rent bikes, take picnics "to go" and head for Ladies or Cisco Beach.

RESTAURANT
Da Paolino, an outdoor restaurant in Capri where you can enjoy delicious seafood and pasta under the canopy of a lemon grove.

MUSEUM
Guggenheim, a captivating interactive experience where you feel like you are inside of a giant nautilus shell while viewing art on the walls. And while you walk in a circular direction, subtly winding around, you're being influenced by the genius of Frank Lloyd Wright.

Self Care

HOBBIES
Treasure hunting, cooking, table-scaping, flower arranging, trip planning, painting, making playlists, entertaining.

PET
Cavalier King Charles Spaniel, the most loving breed of dog I know. Tessa has been with me through thick and thin; she is my shadow. She comes to the office with me every day to follow me around and steal a warmed desk chair. She puts a smile on everyone's face.

FLOWER
Peonies and **rare orchids** are my favorites. Fresh flowers are my not-so-guilty pleasure and, if I'm organized, there are flowers in our home at all times.

INSTRUMENT
I grew up taking **piano** lessons from my friend and teacher Randy Atchinson, who taught me to play by ear. Sitting at the piano, I would lose myself in song. I was never good at reading music, but I can remember every song I played, from *Send in the Clowns* and *The Greatest Love of All* to the *Theme from St. Elmo's Fire*.

SPORTS & ACTIVITIES
Yoga, **Pilates**, **skiing**, **CrossFit**, **kickboxing**. I have my best ideas when there's extra blood flowing to my brain. When I'm feeling blocked, I'll do a headstand and I instantly feel empowered with creativity.

Meaningful Musings

CHERISHED RITUAL
Sunday morning crêpes together as a family. This is my way of keeping the kids engaged and around the table for an hour while we enjoy a sweet and savory breakfast. During summer months, you'll find us outside on the upper boathouse deck.

DREAM DINNER GUESTS
Princess Diana, **Oprah Winfrey**, **Joni Mitchell**, **Dolly Parton**, and **the Dalai Lama**.

MOST MEANINGFUL PIECE OF FURNITURE
My great-grandmother's **American clawfoot mahogany console** with a mirrored back. It was in my grandmother's dining room, and it's been in our living room since we moved to Toronto. I still have memories of my kids sitting on the shelf under it when they were wee ones, staring at themselves while making handprints on the mirror.

MOTTO
My grandmother told my grandfather in church, **"If you can't sing, hum."** Somehow this always resonated as a positive outlook for me and made me realize that a little effort is always worthwhile.

ME IN ONE WORD
Hugger.

MANTRA
I can and I will with love and gratitude.

Wandering the streets of Paris, I'm giddy noticing architectural details and French fashion, but in addition, there are so many amazing indoor venues that are mind-blowing. —AH

HAPPY

HAPPY ROOMS ARE AMONG MY
FAVORITE TO DESIGN. BURSTING
WITH COLOR AND PERSONALITY,
THEY INVITE YOU TO COME IN
AND STAY A WHILE. (AND MAYBE
EVEN INDULGE IN AN IMPROMPTU
DANCE PARTY.)

STEP INSIDE MY FAMILY'S CITY
HOME AND YOU'LL SEE INTO
MY SOUL: IT'S A PLACE WHERE
SATURATED COLORS MINGLE WITH
DRAMATIC PRINTS AND PATTERNS.
A HAPPY HOME MAKES YOU SMILE.

LONDON, ENGLAND 2010

"I'll go to the ends of the earth for the perfect color. To find the right blue for the front door of our Toronto home,
I ran around London with my decks of North American paint colors, trying to match them against doors I liked.
When that didn't work, I went to a U.K. paint store and finally found a perfect match. I love the way this electric
blue pops against the traditional Georgian white door casing—it's made a memorable backdrop for some
treasured family photos, too!"

HOME SWEET HOME

Making a first impression is all about balance, repetition, and symmetry. I used a pair of scalloped Venetian mirrors to mimic the iconic Georgian arch of the door and reinforced that shape with the bench at the base of the stairs. Buy good quality pieces and you can reupholster when you need a change. Part of the fun of decorating is switching it up.

"TO CREATE ONE'S OWN WORLD TAKES COURAGE."

—

GEORGIA O'KEEFFE

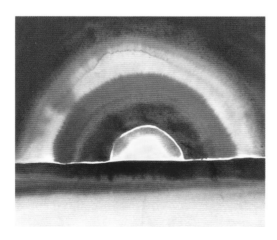

GEORGIA O'KEEFFE, SUNRISE, WATERCOLOR, 1916

I'm never afraid to mix periods and styles, and I've held onto specific pieces that hold deep meaning and memories. The photograph *On the Seine* was taken by Melvin Sokolsky in 1963 for *Harper's Bazaar*. I purchased it in 1998 from Ethelene Staley of the Staley-Wise Gallery in SOHO, and it hung in my single-girl apartment in New York. The sconces flanking the photograph belonged to my husband's German grandmother, who had an appreciation for French furniture. The American Empire mahogany mirror-back pier table beneath came from my grandmother (and her mother before that). All of these things have stayed with me and make me happy.

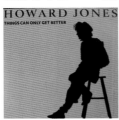  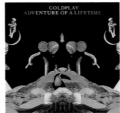

DANCE PARTY PLAYLIST

YOU ARE THE BEST THING
RAY LAMONTAGNE

GROOVE IS IN THE HEART
DEEE-LITE

GET UP OFFA THAT THING
JAMES BROWN

DON'T STOP
FLEETWOOD MAC

GETTIN' JIGGY WIT IT
WILL SMITH

FEELS
PHARREL WILLIAMS,
KATY PERRY, AND BIG SEAN

THINGS CAN ONLY GET BETTER
HOWARD JONES

DANCING ON THE CEILING
LIONEL RICHIE

ADVENTURE OF A LIFETIME
COLD PLAY

VIRTUAL INSANITY
JAMIROQUAI

THE OTHER SIDE
SZA, JUSTIN TIMBERLAKE

SWEET CHILD O' MINE
GUNS & ROSES

DON'T STOP BELIEVIN'
JOURNEY

STAYIN' ALIVE
BEE GEES

DON'T STOP ME NOW
QUEEN

WHAT LOVERS DO
MAROON 5, SZA

PRAISE YOU
KING ARTHUR

I'M COMING OUT
DIANA ROSS

SAY SO
DOJA CAT

CHEAP THRILLS
SIA

RAPPER'S DELIGHT
THE SUGARHILL GANG

Believe it or not, this room is where we spend all our time together as a family. We live in here. It's a musical room, too—we bring in guitars and have weekly jam sessions where we sing and dance with our four kids. All the furniture is super-comfortable and not too formal, so no one feels guilty about sitting on anything.

———

2007

For me, it's important to raise our children in a vibrant environment that inspires joy, happiness, and creativity. Color and pattern encourage them not to take life so seriously, and our home is a laboratory for me to experiment with different combinations. The embroidered Carriacou Pierre Frey fabric on the slipper chairs was the jumping-off point—I fell in love with its boldness and energy and then hunted high and low for the perfect fuchsia velvet on the swivel chair. The multihued circles are from a series by Ulrich Panzer called *Blind Man's Song*, and they represent the merging of the senses and perception of sound, which seemed like a perfect fit for our musical room.

——

The brass-trimmed ostrich leather table is from my furniture line *ah ha!*; it's called 'Amelia,' after my daughter.

—AH

A dining room is about ambiance, sharing stories, and connecting with each other. Shades of blue and purple—from soft amethyst to saturated lapis lazuli—make us all feel content and enveloped when we gather every night for a candlelit dinner.

To create movement and drama in our dining room, I chose this iconic wallpaper by Piero Fornasetti. I've always admired its detailed traditional etchings that somehow feel very modern in a room setting. —AH

From the blue butterflies I bought in Saint Tropez to the rock-crystal cabinet handles and ostrich-leather mirror, these pieces talk to each other and tell a story in ways both visual and energetic. I love mixing high and low. Sparkling brass trim and lacquer are beautifully juxtaposed by matte textures.

When the gallery fills up the wall, it feels like a more purposeful statement.
White mats pull together frames with different finishes.

—

AH

Black, white, and brass: What could be more crisp and glam?
In my office where I multitask, I outlined the drawers in brass
for a playful touch. White grass cloth walls are a luxe backdrop
for a gallery wall of photos that make me happy, from elephants
and fashion to my music hero, Joni Mitchell.

———

Cozy and *plush*—those are the two words I'd use to describe our bedroom. You can see those qualities in the softly pleated ultra-suede headboard, the thick, hand-knotted wool rug, and the Mongolian wool on the acrylic bench at the foot of the bed. No surface is flat; everything has texture and movement. The pièce de résistance is the artwork over the bed by my friend Lori-Ann Bellissimo. It's her interpretation of my husband's and my astrological charts, and it never fails to captivate me with its facets and prisms.

———

My philosophy for kids' rooms? Make them super-happy spaces, understand how they want to feel in their rooms, and involve them in the process. Fully upholstered bed frames are soft, functional, and comfortable when cozying up with a book before bedtime.

———

2011

2012

Happiness is my kids at Halloween. Design and travel are my passions, but coming home is the most joyful feeling of all. I searched for the perfect blue door to satisfy my designer's eye, but seeing my family in front of it gives my work meaning. —AH

2014

2013

2015

2016

2017

2018

2019

WANDERLUST

I'm obsessed with global craftsmanship and anything made by hand. The red grass cloth wallpaper in our little library—also known as "The Red Room"—is a rich backdrop for the many treasures and trinkets we've collected during our travels. I found the suzani on the wall in the Grand Bazaar in **Istanbul**, which perfectly complements the Robert Kime textile I selected for the roman shades. Handwoven baskets from **Ecuador** and **Rwanda** work in harmony with pillows I bought in **India**, while a black Japanese trunk acts as a grounding element. Among my all-time favorite pieces are the lacquer, or Yun-de, trays from **Myanmar** that I discovered on a trip with my mother. Their designs are so elaborate and when I see them, they bring back such vivid memories. Every time I return home from a trip, I'm changed. The people I meet, the landscapes and architecture I admire, and the crafts and culture I absorb expand my mind and fill my soul with gratitude and love.

———

ISTANBUL, 2002

MYANMAR, 1998

ECUADOR, 2012

PERU, 2012

INDIA, 2013

ENGLAND, 2010

INDIA, 2013

MYANMAR, 1998

"RED IS THE GREAT
CLARIFIER—BRIGHT
AND REVEALING.
I CAN'T IMAGINE
BECOMING BORED
WITH RED—IT WOULD
BE LIKE BECOMING
BORED WITH THE
PERSON YOU LOVE."

—

DIANA VREELAND

URBAN PENTHOUSE

Sometimes a killer view dictates the direction of a room; that was the case at this spacious urban oasis. It overlooks both a beautiful park and a twinkling city skyline, so we've brought both of those feelings in with earthy greens, oversized florals, and mixed metals. Sisal is my go-to backdrop to give any room an organic quality. It acts as a grounding factor for a light and airy two-tiered acrylic table—an interactive tablescaping venue for my client to curate her beloved coffee table books, collected baskets, beads, candles, and flower arrangements.

The diptych by Canadian artist Kathryn Macnaughton makes a graphic statement. Believe it or not, these two paintings were the last piece of the puzzle. I asked my client, Justine Deluce, to join me at the Art Toronto show, and we both fell in love with these pieces as we bonded with the artist over a shared admiration for the abstract expressionist Helen Frankenthaler. It seems like we designed the room around the paintings, but they were an end-of-process find—a serendipitous moment and treasured memory.

"THERE ARE NO RULES. THAT IS HOW ART IS BORN, HOW BREAKTHROUGHS HAPPEN. GO AGAINST THE RULES OR IGNORE THE RULES. THAT IS WHAT INVENTION IS ABOUT."

—
HELEN FRANKENTHALER

Every white kitchen needs a special customized focal point, so I designed the white oak X-chevron hood. The Lenny Kravitz–designed black leather and brass stools give the island the edge I was looking for.

From Colombia to my client's cabinets,
I'm always finding ways to integrate
treasures from my travels. —AH

In this open-concept kitchen, the feature of the dining area is the Nigel's Tartan Hermès wallpaper, a large-scale, modern interpretation of a classic Scottish plaid. It's graphic and architectural from far away—like the view of downtown through floor-to-ceiling windows—but has the softness of a watercolor painting up close. The effect is both casual and dressy—like wearing jeans with a great pair of heels. Placing a channeled banquette in front of the graphic wallpaper is like composing music; there's a rhythm to keep in mind. Had it just been a tight-back banquette, the grouping would have lost the beat and fallen flat.

———

COLOMBIA

Our family visited this lively and lush country in 2018. From the beautiful seaside UNESCO World Heritage site of Cartagena to the vibrant city of Medellín, the Coffee Triangle in the Andes Mountains, and the bustling city of Bogotá, Colombia has a culture rich in art, architecture, food, and design. Here are a few of my favorite memories.

CARTAGENA

In Cartagena, colonial chic meets Caribbean flair; the old city walls and fortresses bear witness to gold treasures, pirates and battles. Cartagena was one of the first towns to proclaim independence from Spain in 1810.

While strolling the streets at dusk, I breathe the salted air as playful salsa trails from a second-floor window. I admire flourishing bougainvillea adorning the vibrant façades with quaint Spanish colonial balcony railing and terracotta roofs. I find myself obsessing not only over the doors, but the door knockers. I think to myself: This is the magic that inspired Gabríel Garcia Márquez.

Enjoying a sundowner at Café Del Mar overlooking the historic city walls, we let our gaze wander over the Caribbean Sea.

MOCHILA BAGS

Authentic woven pieces by the indigenous women of the Wayuu tribe from La Guajira, Colombia, each Wayuu bag is a unique piece of art and takes about one month to complete.

MEDELLÍN

Once dubbed "The Most Dangerous City in the World" by *Time* magazine due to the drug-fueled violence of Pablo Escobar, Medellín has undergone a transformation in the last 20 years. In addition to big improvements in public safety, there's been a huge surge in urban development projects, including Colombia's first metro system and cable cars to service poorer neighborhoods located high on the mountainsides, as well as new parks and libraries.

The natural beauty and unique climate of Medellín is something

to behold. Set 4,905 feet above sea level in a valley surrounded by tall green mountains, its proximity to the equator ensures constant spring-like temperatures year-round.

COMUNA 13

Astounding graffiti art. Once one of the most dangerous neighborhoods in Medellín, the Comuna 13 clings to the mountainside above the San Javier metro station. It has undergone an impressive transformation in recent times and is now considered safe to visit. The *escaleras eléctricas*, six sets of orange outdoor escalators, provide access to incredible murals and graffiti, overlooking views of the surrounding hillsides covered in small local homes.

PLAZA BOTERO AND PARQUE BERRÍO

Home to 23 of Fernando Botero's larger-than-life sculptures, this plaza can be reached via the Parque Berrío metro station.

Across the street from Plaza Botero, this small park is always filled with juice vendors and local street performers playing traditional Colombian music.

PEREIRA

One of the three areas that make up the Coffee Triangle is Pereira in the Andes. The region is noted for the steep-sloped valleys (rich in volcanic soil) that make much of the area quite difficult to reach, while the hot and rainy climate is ideal for cultivating the best smooth Arabica coffee.

COCORA VALLEY

The Cocora Valley is one of the most beautiful and surreal places in Colombia. The valley is home to the tallest palm trees in the world, the Quindío wax palm, which can reach 196 feet tall. They stand like sentinels, alone in the wide, green-carpeted valley, and have a whimsical, wonky appearance like something out of a Dr. Seuss book.

Build a frame of millwork around a sofa for instant architectural interest. The den does not have windows, so the photograph mounted in the center acts as a portal into the natural world. Multiple light sources help to soften the mood and add ambiance.

——

Fresh flowers are mesmerizing, like staring into a fire. I'm captivated by their personalities, colors, and textures.

—AH

As a child, I remember thumbing through my mother's forbidden drawer of perfectly folded Hermès silk scarves. I wanted nothing more than to pull them all out and study the pattern, color, and intricate design of each one. —AH

An urban jungle with flowers, shrubs, and fountains comes alive, thanks to Jardin D'Osier wallpaper by Pierre Marie for Hermès. The teal colorway is fresh, so I paired the wallpaper with marigold chairs, which speak to the cognac-colored leather side tables and brass accents.

Inspired by tailored Chanel bags and boxes, I've outlined rooms in grosgrain ribbon before—why not use strips of black metal in the bathroom? We mapped out large porcelain marble slabs to line up the veins, then accentuated the seams with black metal. Similar to highlighting seam lines on a couture dress, I've created delineation, depth, dimension, and contrast with black metal.

——

When you're inventing something, the process can have its trials and tribulations. But if you don't take risks, you never create something new. —AH

SITTING PRETTY

Dining rooms are for making memories. Use the good china and stemware. Pull out the silverware. Light candles. And not just when company's coming. Fine items with patina become even more beautiful since they've been used and loved. Of course, it doesn't hurt when the space is fabulous and welcoming—a black lacquered Jansen dining table, Biedermeier chest, and geometric rug set the stage for special nights with family and friends.

ANNE'S BACON-WRAPPED WATER CHESTNUTS

This is my most requested hors d'oeuvre Chez Hepfer—enjoy!

2 CANS	WHOLE WATER CHESTNUTS
1 LB	BACON
½ CUP	BROWN SUGAR
¼ CUP	MAYONNAISE
¼ CUP	SRIRACHA SAUCE
3 TBSP	LOW-SODIUM SOY SAUCE

1. **PRE-HEAT** broiler to 400 degrees.

2. **COOK** bacon in frying pan over medium heat until soft but not crisp. Cut in half on diagonal, then wrap each piece around a water chestnut and secure with a toothpick.

3. **PLACE** bacon bundles on broiler pan covered in tin foil.

4. **MIX** brown sugar, mayonnaise, Sriracha, and soy together. Spoon half over the bacon bundles and broil until bacon is cooked to satisfaction.

5. **FLIP** bacon bundles and cook other side.

6. **PLACE** finished bundles in casserole dish and spoon remaining sauce over top. Reheat when ready to serve.

Watermelon-pink velvet tufted settees give this gracious room a sense of symmetry—not to mention an extra place to perch with a cocktail. Pleated draperies with holdbacks infuse the space with the feeling of a modern French salon.

———

This kitchen-family room has the feeling of a sunroom, and it needed that wow moment of ikat pattern to fill the corner. My client said yes to bullion fringe on the banquette—a traditional decorator detail—but we balanced it with the iconic mid-century modern Tulip table and chairs by Eero Saarinen for a happy-chic mix of preppy and friendly. ChiChi, my furry friend, thinks so, too.

———

THE MIDTOWN MULE

This refreshing cocktail is my own invention. Sip at the end of a long day or to kick off the weekend in style!

1 ½ OZ
AMARO NONINO

1 ½ OZ
DOMAINE DE CANTON
(FRENCH GINGER LIQUEUR)

1 ½ OZ
BOURBON

1 ½ OZ
STRAINED LEMON JUICE

SHAKE and strain over ice.

Upholstered walls give a master
bedroom a luxurious, sound-
dampened soothing quality for
a good night's sleep. I selected
"Breakwater," a hand-printed
linen by Christopher Farr, for
a painterly quality on the walls.

"NEVER MAKE A BIG DECISION WITHOUT SLEEPING ON IT."

—

MARTHA STEWART

When a bedroom is draped in soft folds and pleats, and wrapped in
a soothing, watery palette, it's the epitome of a personal retreat.
White adds crisp contrast, while gold accents warm up the otherwise cool palette.

———

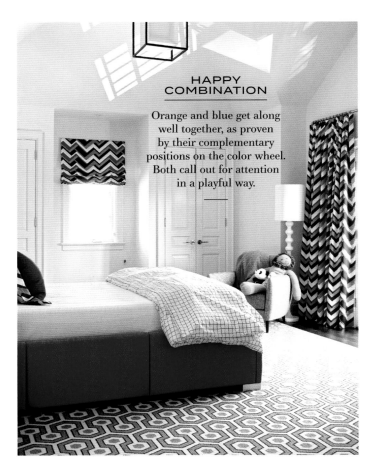

HAPPY COMBINATION

Orange and blue get along well together, as proven by their complementary positions on the color wheel. Both call out for attention in a playful way.

———

Orange-striped fabric reminds me of sun and salt air under a cheery beach umbrella in Positano, Italy. I designed these headboards to resemble surf boards, complete with nautical lights.

Orange livens up a room like no other color.
Of course, it has to be the right orange:
A cheerful shade with enough richness
and depth to feel sophisticated.

—AH

RELAXED

ESCAPING TO NATURE CLEANSES THE SOUL, QUIETS THE MIND, AND ALLOWS US TO FOCUS ON THE THINGS THAT WE ENJOY.

WHETHER IT'S A COTTAGE, CABIN, OR COUNTRY HOUSE, THESE SPECIAL RETREATS INVITE US TO RECLAIM OUR LEISURE TIME, CREATE SPECIAL MEMORIES WITH FAMILY AND FRIENDS, AND RECONNECT WITH OURSELVES SURROUNDED BY BIG SKY AND MESMERIZING SUNSETS.

IT'S TIME TO HIT THE PAUSE BUTTON AND CONTEMPLATE LIFE, LOVE, AND THE LAID-BACK MOMENTS WE CHERISH.

NORTHERN HAVEN

I wanted a home with a deep relationship to nature. At our cottage in Ontario's rugged Muskoka region, the air is pure, fresh, and balmy. Everyone swears they never sleep better than when they're here, enveloped by nature's sights, sounds, and smells. In the morning, the experience of sipping a steaming coffee and looking out at the lake is nothing short of meditative, and a ritual I enjoy all year long through the changing seasons.

The building nods to the gracious old cottages of the Muskoka region, but I gave it a modern, Belgian-inspired feel with black windows, clear white oak floors, and a neutral palette so as to not deflect from the natural beauty outside. As an interior designer, I spend my days looking at color, texture, and pattern, so creating this minimal, unpretentious environment is a refuge from the visual stimulation that comes with my work. For our family of six, the cottage has to be comfortable and low-key—every piece has a role to play in fulfilling those goals.

I was here every week as the cottage was built, marveling at shadows created by the rising and setting sun, and studying the direction of the shifting breezes. Working with our stonemason and master carpenters, I oversaw every detail and appreciate the true craftsmanship in every mitered corner, floating shelf, and barn beam. Now, when the doors slide open in summer and I can smell the pine trees, see light dancing on the water, and hear the sounds of kids jumping off the dock—it's just as I envisioned.

A giant picture window frames the magnificent views of soaring white pines with the lake beyond. The sliding doors to the upper deck pocket behind the fireplace, opening up and unifying the great room with nature.

To achieve a peaceful space and sense of calm, I exercised restraint, focusing on monochromatic tones of oatmeal and flax, as well as white linen, to contrast with the black windows. With a restricted palette, textures come into sharper focus. I layered mixed metals and various natural, rustic materials: linen, leather, woven rattan, Mongolian wool, reclaimed wood, and granite. Texture also comes from the handmade pieces I collect, like earthenware pottery or the set of Indian paper cuttings that flank the oversized Balinese shell mirror on the wall opposite the fireplace.

I bought the paper cuttings in Agra, India, which replicate the marble patterns in the screens of the Taj Mahal. I shadowbox-framed them with different earthy-toned linen backgrounds. —AH

The ceiling beams, woven French wicker armchairs, and oak floor infuse the space with the calm of the natural world through color and texture. The industrial light fixture and concrete tabletop maintain this impression with stony hues, and also offer modern character.

——

"A HOUSE IS MUCH MORE THAN A SHELTER, IT SHOULD LIFT US EMOTIONALLY AND SPIRITUALLY."

—

JOHN SALADINO

Three pairs of French doors on either side of the dining room face the lake and garden, respectively. The reclaimed beams above connect pilasters and columns; these also separate the doors and provide architectural continuity. Retractable screens are hidden inside the pilasters for functionality and a streamlined look.

—

With four children, we spend a lot of time in our kitchen. I wanted to design a room that was as appealing as any other in the cottage—a place that would draw people in. I paired pale-gray base cabinets and durable white Caesarstone counters with a cerused oak island. Natural light does all the work of making it a serene environment, even on a busy day.

———

MOM'S BLUEBERRY TART WITH SHORTBREAD CRUST

I grew up enjoying this sweet treat—one of my mom's classic recipes. It's like a slice of summer on your plate.

FOR SHORTBREAD CRUST:

1 ¼ CUP	FLOUR
⅛ TSP	SALT
2 TBSP	WHITE SUGAR
½ CUP	UNSALTED BUTTER, SOFTENED (1 STICK)
½ TBSP	WHITE VINEGAR

1. PREHEAT oven to 400 degrees.

2. MIX ingredients by cutting butter into dry ingredients with a pastry blender. Mixture should resemble coarse crumbs.

3. SPRINKLE mixture with vinegar and shape into dough with lightly floured fingers and press evenly into a springform pan to quarter-inch thickness.

4. ALLOW enough dough around edge to ensure filling is contained, about ½" high.

FOR FILLING:

5 CUPS	FRESH BLUEBERRIES (WILD, IF POSSIBLE)
2 TBSP	FLOUR
⅔ CUP	WHITE SUGAR
⅛ TSP	CINNAMON

1. MIX 3 cups blueberries with above ingredients and pour evenly on top of pastry crust.

2. BAKE on bottom rack in oven at 400 degrees 50 to 60 minutes, until crust is brown and filling bubbly.

3. REMOVE from oven and cool on a baking rack.

4. SPRINKLE evenly with remaining 2 cups fresh blueberries.

5. SERVE with vanilla ice cream or whipped cream.

The U-shaped banquette is loungy and comfortable enough to pack in our large family and guests around two large tables—we've accommodated up to 20 people. We have a ritual Sunday breakfast where I flip crêpes at the table. Note the floor outlet for accessible plug-ins. On winter evenings, we gather around the fondue pot.

The den is where we cozy up with a bowl of popcorn to watch movies. Reclaimed barnboard on the walls and ceiling creates a feeling of enclosure and intimacy while still connecting to the open flow of the house. Texture plays a part again here—the walls are rough, the cushions are soft cashmere, the table is chiseled, and the floors are sleek. My husband and I bought Nick Brandt's *Giraffes* years before we visited Africa; now the piece brings back memories of our safari in Kenya.

The windows in the sunroom, tucked away in the corner of the house, drop down into the knee wall below, allowing the space to transform into a screened-in porch. I designed the drum shade from thick-gauge screen material with filament bulbs, and it hangs over a black-stained oak coffee table. Upholstered swivel chairs allow you to turn and take in the views, while woven leather chairs by South African designer John Vogel act as pieces of art.

Our entrance is minimal yet warm and showcases a connection to nature. For the staircase, I chose a glass rail with oak treads on an iron-steel stringer—the open stairs allow light to pass through and reveal a view of the garden beyond.

———

I designed a farmhouse trestle table made from reclaimed hemlock to capture a rustic spirit for the powder room off the entry. The mirror is made from the same wood but stained gray for interest.

———

When you surround a bedroom with windows, it's like sleeping in the trees. Because our principal bedroom faces west, it gets gorgeous late-afternoon sun and mesmerizing views of the sunset. Here, I played with a mix of materials—a woven mat bench from Borneo, a petrified wood table with a nickel base, vintage lamps, a hide rug—that are unified by their warm, calming hues. Hand-applied plaster gives the walls a sense of texture and history.

My goal for the principal bath was to mimic the feeling of a lake landscape with the large stone-shaped tub and warm oatmeal–tiled walls and floor. The vanity—a nod to a mid-century-style credenza—echoes the color of the tree trunks outside the window.

——

Reclaimed-wood shelves are home to my collection of African headrests, hand-carved soapstone sculptures, and baskets. —AH

Painting is a meditation for me.
I lose myself in a view and in my palette.
If only I had more time to paint...
—
AH

For a family of six, this is one of the hardest-working rooms in the house (and it never looks this tidy). I'm sure you can imagine why!

———

The simplicity of this room calls attention to the beachy striped fabric, honey-colored vintage caned beds, which complement the oak floor, and the feather-dart mirror shaped like the sun.

The boys' ensuite is crisp and nautical with classic shiplap walls and a striped rug to match the one in the bedroom.

"GIVE THE ONES YOU
LOVE WINGS TO FLY,
ROOTS TO COME BACK,
AND REASONS TO STAY."

—

THE DALAI LAMA

"HOW BEAUTIFULLY LEAVES GROW OLD. HOW FULL OF LIGHT AND COLOR ARE THEIR LAST DAYS."

—

JOHN BURROUGHS

The portrait of Amelia was a gift from our nanny, Olive, who commissioned her friend to do the pencil drawing.

DOCK TUNES PLAYLIST

LOVELY DAY
BILL WITHERS

THE TIDE IS HIGH
BLONDIE

ISLANDS IN THE STREAM
DOLLY PARTON & KENNY ROGERS

JAMMING
BOB MARLEY & THE WAILERS

GOLDEN HOUR
KACEY MUSGRAVES

SAY SOMETHING
JUSTIN TIMBERLAKE,
CHRIS STAPLETON

IN THE COLORS
BEN HARPER &
THE INNOCENT CRIMINALS

FREE FALLIN'
JOHN MAYER

FOREVER IN BLUE JEANS
NEIL DIAMOND

YELLOW EYES
RAYLAND BAXTER

**YOU ARE THE SUNSHINE
OF MY LIFE**
STEVIE WONDER

MEANT TO BE
BEBE REXHA,
FLORIDA GEORGIA LINE

FROM EDEN
HOZIER

BOA SORTE
VANESSA DA MATA, BEN HARPER

SOUTHERN SUN
BOY & BEAR

IT'S FIVE O'CLOCK SOMEWHERE
ALAN JACKSON & JIMMY BUFFET

WAGON WHEEL
DARIUS RUCKER

DANCING IN THE MOONLIGHT
TOP LOADER

SUMMER BREEZE
JASON MRAZ

THESE ARE THE DAYS
VAN MORRISON

DROPS OF JUPITER
TRAIN

The boathouse deck is where we live in the summer. Nothing is too polished or high maintenance, since it's a place for wet bathing suits, easy lunches, and coffee or lemonade breaks. An antique Balinese table looks better each year with age, while a driftwood mirror acts as a window and reflects the view. The chevron upholstery, a Schumacher fabric, is a modern play on waves.

———

SHREDDED SESAME CHICKEN & CUCUMBER

Refreshing and filling—perfect for a dockside lunch.

6 CUPS	CUCUMBER JULIENNED IN STRIPS
4 WHOLE	CHICKEN BREASTS, SKINNED AND BONED
4 TSP	CORNSTARCH
2	EGG WHITES (BEATEN LIGHTLY)
2 TBSP	DRY SHERRY, DIVIDED
2 TSP	SALT
1 TSP	WHITE PEPPER
	PEANUT OIL FOR DEEP FRYING
¼ CUP	SESAME OIL
3 TBSP	TOASTED SESAME SEEDS
3	GREEN ONIONS (FINELY CHOPPED), OPTIONAL
¼ CUP	CILANTRO (FINELY CHOPPED), OPTIONAL

1. REMOVE seeds from cucumbers, julienne in thin strips and place in refrigerator to keep cold.

2. PLACE chicken on a flat surface and slice it thin on the bias. Shred the slices as fine as possible. (This is easier if the meat is partially frozen before slicing and the slices stacked before shredding).

3. USING fingers, blend the shredded chicken with the corn starch, egg white, 1 tbsp of sherry and salt. Refrigerate for 30 minutes.

4. IN A WOK or large frying pan, heat oil. When it is warm but not piping hot add the chicken mixture.

5. COOK stirring, just until the shreds separate and the chicken is cooked through.

6. DRAIN on paper towels and put in the refrigerator.

7. WHEN COOL, mix together with cucumbers. Add sesame oil.

8. ADD more salt if necessary.

9. KEEP refrigerated until serving. Serve on cold plates. Top with toasted sesame seeds, and if you wish, chopped green onion and/or chopped cilantro.

SOUTH AFRICA

I've had a beautiful connection with South Africa for many years. Not only is my ostrich-leather furniture line, *ah ha!*, manufactured in this vast country, we've been honored to support township schools outside of Cape Town. Giving back has been a fundamental goal of my company, and it's been wonderful to have an impact on children in need. South African history has also been deeply impactful as we watched Nelson Mandela lead people through the terrible times of apartheid. In the face of all that, the people of South Africa have retained their unwavering warmth, creativity, and hope for a bright future. Sweeping vistas, cliffside coastal drives, lush farms and vineyards, and bustling cities are vivid images in my travel memory bank.

WESTERN CAPE
The Grootbos Lodge is a small, special eco retreat where you can hike, ride horses and bikes, and be at one with nature as you explore caves, walk beaches, and marvel over the 2,500 hectares of 800 plant and flower species of the Fynbos—a small belt of natural vegetation. Walking through Fynbos and taking in the otherworldly smell, I was happy to spot one of my favorite flower species, the protea, in its natural habitat. The coast is magical and rugged. I will also mention that I went on my first (and last!) shark cage dive with my kids here.

CAPE TOWN
Cape Town's Kloof Street is a marvel of graffiti art, antique stores, and interior design shops. There's a fabulous market at the Victoria & Alfred Waterfront that carries everything from food to African crafts and all things handmade. Touring Robben Island and seeing Mandela's jail cell was an emotional experience that gave us insight into the brutality of apartheid and the courage of those who sacrificed everything to defeat it.

CLANWILLIAM, CEDERBERG
About a four-hour drive north of Cape Town, there is a very special small lodge resort and game reserve called Bushman's Kloof. The cozy farmhouse is nestled in the foothills of the Cederberg Mountains, among open plains where you can view Cape Mountain zebras, Gemsbok South African oryx, bontebok, red hartebeest, grey rhebok and ostriches. It is also the home of an archaeological treasure: 130 prehistoric rock art paintings by the indigenous San people, some dating back 10,000 years.

WINE COUNTRY
Don't miss Babylonstoren, one of the oldest Cape Dutch farms in the Franschhoek wine valley, where the shops sell local delicacies, homewares, and hand-printed linens. One of South Africa's most inspiring sculptors is Dylan Lewis. Visit his sculpture garden in Stellenbosch to see his creations come to life as you journey a four-kilometer path. Check out Corinne de Hass's ceramic studio, where you'll find gorgeous pieces that will make your heart sing! I'm seriously obsessed.

JOHANNESBURG
I spent a day with artist James Delaney, who toured me around the Circa Gallery and smaller galleries and design stores along Keys Art Mile. We then checked out the Westcliffe Steps, Maboneng, and the Victoria Yards, where James showed me his studio. You'll find great stores at 44 Stanley, and my favorite of all was Kim Sacks, which has an amazing collection of contemporary and tribal pieces. Walk around Constitution Hill, the site of some of South Africa's most pivotal moments. Be prepared for an emotional, heart-wrenching visit to the Apartheid Museum.

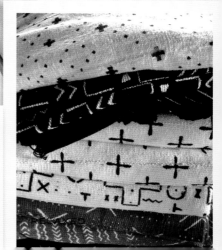

LAKE ROSSEAU BLUES

THE ARRIVAL

The shimmer of sun on water, the sound of waves lapping at the dock, the smell of summer—those senses are embedded in every cottager's soul.

Arriving on Friday night and leaving your cares behind is like one big exhale.

Time to relax, unwind, and, most importantly, breathe.

Is there a more perfect place to drink in summer's splendor than a boathouse? With doors open wide and fresh air flowing through, this serene two-bedroom space brings lake and sky indoors. Taking my cues from nature, I proposed a clean and fresh blue-and-white palette against a whitewashed interior that draws the eye up to the 20-foot ceilings. Floating back-to-back sofas in the middle of a room ground the space and provide an abundance of seating for admiring the 180-degree views. The great room represents easy, breezy living at its best.

——

The overscale French-bistro-style gooseneck lights that attach to either end of the island were designed as a solution—peaked ceilings make it difficult to successfully suspend pendants. Instead, these polished nickel lights provide directional task lighting, bring symmetry and balance to the kitchen, and enhance the sense of loftiness.

——

Making a blue-and-white palette feel current is an artful process. I love to combine unusual shades, like cornflower and periwinkle, and choose modern shapes and contours for the furniture to keep the overall design clean and crisp.

——

We pushed the envelope by adding a bay window and
built-in banquette to gain immersive views for summer
dining. The table is topped in zinc and finished off with
nailheads. Chunky woven seagrass chairs inject some
warmth into the cool, watery color scheme.

"THAT IT WILL NEVER COME AGAIN IS WHAT MAKES LIFE SO SWEET."

—
EMILY DICKINSON

Clean and simple are the hallmarks of the guest room. The upholstered bed frames have a storage drawer hidden in the footboard, and the headboards are stepped to frame the window. The blue striated dresser and unadorned white walls give the eye a breather and keep the space feeling crisp—the Peter Dunham pattern on the beds provides a touch of interest and movement.

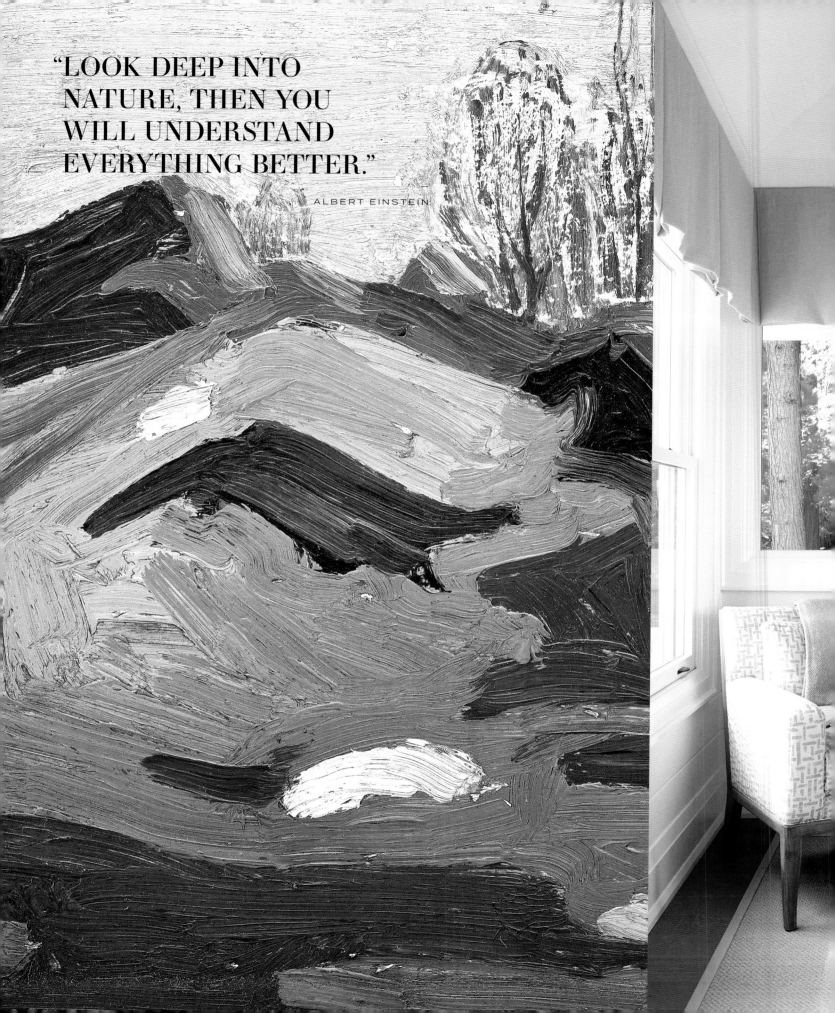

"LOOK DEEP INTO NATURE, THEN YOU WILL UNDERSTAND EVERYTHING BETTER."

ALBERT EINSTEIN

High ceilings call for big ideas. A custom headboard becomes an art installation, especially when upholstered in a fabric that resembles an impressionist painting by one of the Canadian Group of Seven, who were inspired by the light and landscape of lake country. The row of tailored valances are mounted at the horizontal line where wall meets ceiling, tricking the eye into believing the windows are taller than they are. Soft shades of sky and lilac are pulled from the painterly bed frame fabric for a serene and soothing effect.

Varied wood tones and geometric prints pop against a charcoal exterior wall, creating an inviting outdoor space for curling up with a morning coffee or pre-dinner aperitif.

BLISTERED SHISHITO PEPPERS WITH SWEET SRIRACHA MAYO

This is the easiest snack to serve guests on the dock with margaritas—an incredible flavor combination.

1 TBSP	MAYONNAISE
1 TBSP	SRIRACHA SAUCE
1 TSP	THAI SWEET CHILI SAUCE
1 TBSP	AVOCADO OIL
8 OZ	SHISHITO PEPPERS
2 TBSP	LOW-SODIUM SOY SAUCE

1. MIX mayonnaise, Sriracha, and Thai sauce together. Refrigerate until ready to serve.

2. HEAT avocado oil over medium-high heat in large pan.

3. FRY shishito peppers for 10 minutes, turning gently with tongs to blister sides.

4. PLACE in serving bowl and drizzle with low-sodium soy sauce.

5. SERVE with dipping sauce.

LOOKOUT PEAK

This retreat, with its elevation on a hill above the lake, feels more like a luxe lodge than a typical cottage or cabin. My clients embraced the idea of rustic materials that are inherent in the environment, so we celebrated locally quarried granite and reclaimed hemlock for the floors throughout. Getting the right shades for both was incredibly important—we wanted a monotone, medium gray for the granite and rich hemlock stained to downplay the natural red.

This space was an addition to the existing building, where we incorporated retractable doors and screens. The indoor-outdoor dining area is truly at one with nature, bringing back fond memories of camp cabins and country barns. The fully barnboard-clad walls and ceiling introduce a sense of drama and mystery to the property.

—

We uplit the ceiling so it would glow softly at night and melt into the night sky during cozy candlelit dinners or rousing rounds of board games. Though there are many spectacular spaces here, this is the go-to gathering spot.

—

A restrained use of pattern and materials for the furnishings allows the barnboard and granite to remain the singular "wow" moment.

———

Salvaged barnboard plays a starring role throughout the space. There's something special about incorporating beams and boards that have been weathered to the perfect shade of gray and lovingly repurposed from old barns in the region. It takes the skill of a master carpenter to seam the pieces together properly, but the result looks effortless.

———

Separating the dining room and the great room, the back-to-back fireplaces are a grounding feature. Here, I selected a variation of granite colors and tones to create movement and character. All the stones are randomly cut but deliberately laid out to infuse both the dining and living areas with authentic character.

My goal with this project was to create a bridge between indoors and outdoors. The subtle palette showcases rustic textures and local materials to create Zen-like harmony. —AH

In the bar area, millwork was stained gray to complement the natural tones of the reclaimed barnboard. Rope detailing on the ceiling fixture adds a rustic twist.

———

Minimal decoration in the principal bedroom ensures comfort without sacrificing the magnificent views. Gray sisal carpet plays off the stone palette and infuses found-in-nature texture. A touch of black via oiled bronze sconces gives the room contrast.

———

Though simple in appearance, the principal bath is design intensive. We framed the vanity in white Caesarstone, counter-mounted vessel sinks, and installed faucets and sconces atop the mirror, which extends to the ceiling and is framed in the same barnboard as the drawer fronts. All of these techniques open up the room and create a feeling of spaciousness and serenity.

———

A find from an antique shop, this woven wicker mid-century chair had a wonderful shape but needed some TLC. We sprayed it black and added a cute seat cushion for a good-as-new look. The two framed feather prints speak to one another, inviting nature inside and offering a meditation of their variations.

———

The guest room bed frame offered the perfect spot for one of my favorite fabrics by Brooklyn-based designer Michele Dopp. The delicate Xs remind me of stars in the evening sky. John Robshaw pillows feel almost like a reverse of the bed upholstery. The finishing detail? Black piping that delineates the headboard from the white wall.

———

You can't go wrong with a great stripe. I love to railroad fabric to create horizontal lines even if the print isn't oriented that way. The walls are clad in 7-inch shiplap board with a ¼-inch square reveal, which is one of my signature elements for cottage design. It's important to use clear, rough-sawn pine so there are no knots, but you can still see the texture of the grain beneath the paint.

———

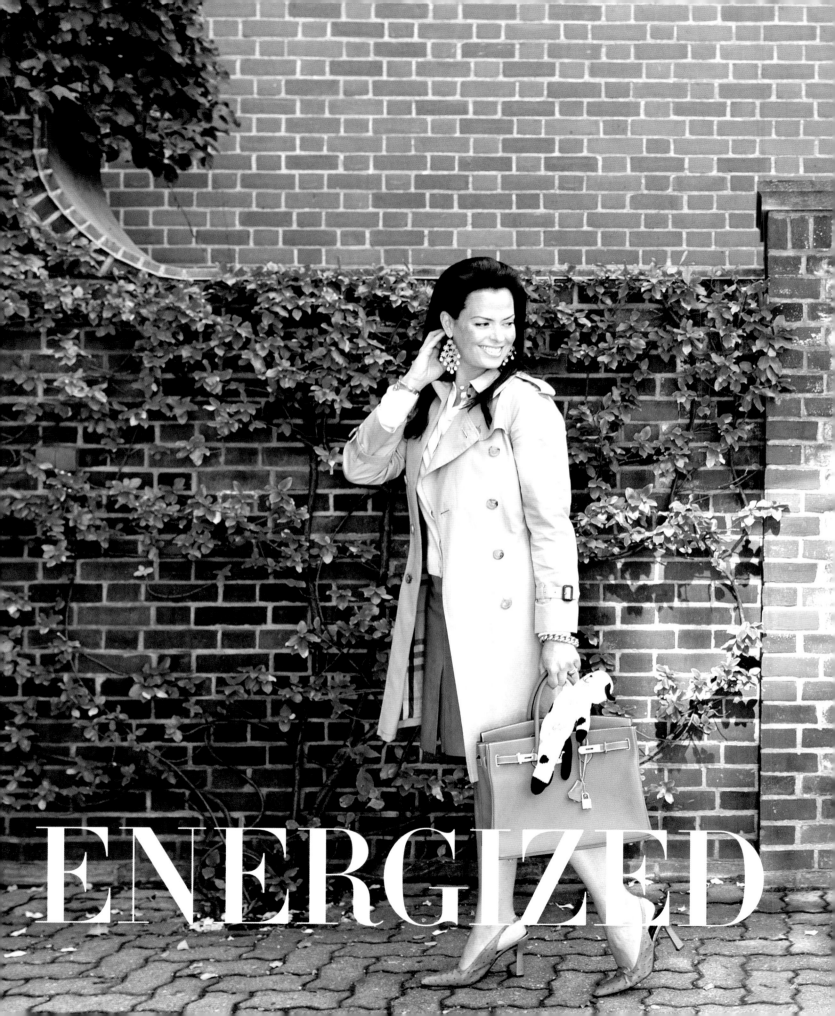

ENERGIZED

I'M A BIG BELIEVER THAT ENERGY COMES FROM ALL AROUND, FROM NATURE TO COLOR, AND IT'S A LIFE FORCE THAT OPENS US UP AND NUDGES US FORWARD. WE CAN DIAL IT UP OR TURN IT DOWN. PATTERN, SCALE, AND SHAPES CREATE MOVEMENT, WHICH IS A TYPE OF ENERGY ALL ITS OWN.

TAPPING INTO THOSE ENERGY SOURCES—ZESTY PALETTES, NATURAL METALS, AND CHAKRA-CLEARING STONES—HELPS ME TRUST MY GUT WHILE I PLAN THE ELEMENTS OF A ROOM.

I OFTEN HEAR MY CLIENTS' VOICES IN MY HEAD LIVESTREAMING THEIR PREFERENCES AND WISH LISTS AS I PIECE TOGETHER THE ELEMENTS OF A THREE-DIMENSIONAL SPACE.

POLISHED GEM

This isn't your typical neighborhood house. The cool young family who lives here had just returned from living abroad, so our idea was to infuse the spaces with energy via unpredictable combinations of juicy colors and a play on outlines, geometry, and contrast. Recurring motifs create fluid transitions from room to room, including several eye-catching nods to Italy, the couple's cherished getaway spot.

Using black in a room is a choreographed dance. Here, the black lines in the Serge Mouille light fixture, the picture frame, and the roman shades accentuate the fragmented linear design of the rug, which I designed based on a Moroccan pattern enlarged in scale. To give the black depth, I played with contrasting matte and polished finishes.

———

Layering texture is key to amping up a room's energy. Tactile, chalky cork wall coverings from Phillip Jeffries sparkle thanks to gold-leaf flecks embedded in the cork. For unexpected contrast, we covered the door leading to the black-lacquered media room in black leather, and finished it off with brass nailhead diagonal stripes.

———

Green is the color of life and growth—soothing to the eye, with a deep and penetrating hum. I designed a curved, emerald velvet sofa, so luxurious and enveloping for entertaining, and used it as the grounding element for one seating area in front of the fireplace. The artwork over the fire is by Donald Baechler.

———

You'd think black would make a room feel smaller, but instead the walls seem to expand and feel infinite—like the night sky. —AH

There's nothing better than a cozy and beautifully appointed den or family room that feels luxurious and elevates the experience of something as simple as watching a movie together. The custom hand-knotted rug is an homage to one of my favorite semiprecious stones, malachite. Playing with geometry, I designed the tricolored needlepoint for the three lumbar pillows.

MALACHITE

Since the 17th century, this naturally occurring
mineral has been a talisman of health and
happiness. The stone was named for its
resemblance to the leaves of the mallow plant
and is the oldest known green pigment to be used
in Egyptian tomb paintings. For me, its repetitive
pattern is mesmerizing and when I see a malachite
piece on my travels, I snap it up. Once, in
Cape Town, South Africa, I stopped in my tracks
to buy a pair of malachite obelisks, knowing
I'd regret it if I didn't. Beautiful and organic,
malachite accents—whether in printed textiles
or the stone itself—bring a wonderful,
meditative energy to any space.

———

Custom malachite pieces for the faucet and cabinet handles make this powder room even more of a jewel box.

A hand-painted malachite mural by artist Peter Allerton gives this foyer a rich, painterly quality.

For the entryway and staircase of my clients' forever home, I proposed custom, hand-painted de Gournay wallpaper with a silver-leaf background that's whimsical and pretty. The traditional chinoiserie design infuses the space with elegance, but the silvery background feels fresh and modern. —AH

A double-height installation up to the second story emphasizes the sense of organic airiness and grandeur. The plants and flowering trees are climbing up the walls. Dolomite marble floors and white wainscoting were kept purposefully quiet to let the de Gournay stand on its own.

——

I get a kick out of bending design rules from time to time. Here, we cut the paper and pasted it over the door trim, so the flowers appear to creep over the millwork to create a glamorous, secret-garden effect.

——

For a personal touch, we added each family member's monogram in a secret spot within the landscape. You'll find yourself treasure hunting within the wallpaper's fine details.

———

Inspired by Roman geometric floors, I chose an iconic rhombus-pattern tile to extend from the mudroom into the kitchen, to unite both spaces. The floor is made from three colors of marble and all the pieces were hand-cut. The size felt right and balanced the scales between traditional and modern. Diner-style swivel stools upholstered with faux-lizard-textured leather give the room a rich accent.

Detail of floor in the Villa Aurelia,
American Academy in Rome.

You can never have enough storage space when there
are kids in the house (trust me, I know). The key is to
maximize closed storage in every nook and cranny
to ensure clutter stays out of sight.

——

So many clients ask for built-in breakfast nooks and I'm happy to oblige. A tight-back upholstered banquette with loungy lumbar cushions makes a kitchen comfy and inviting for lazy weekend brunches. —AH

ZUCCHINI STEAMED WITH AMALFI COAST SHRIMP WITH MINT & LEMON SAUCE

I learned to make this dish during a visit to Ravello, on the Amalfi Coast; this is my own take on a memorable meal.

6 MEDIUM	ZUCCHINIS
1 TBSP	EXTRA VIRGIN OLIVE OIL, DIVIDED
1 TSP	MINCED GARLIC, DIVIDED
1 TSP	MINCED FRESH MINT, DIVIDED
¼ CUP	LEMON JUICE
1 CUP PLUS 2 TBSP	FISH OR VEGETABLE BROTH, DIVIDED
2 LARGE	RAW, DEVEINED, PEELED SHRIMP
	CRACKED PEPPER
	SEA SALT
1	LEMON CUT IN WEDGES
	THINLY SLICED TOASTED BREAD

1. **HALVE** zucchinis lengthwise. Cut off ends. Cut out half of white pulp and discard. Julienne remaining zucchini into thin sticks. Put aside.

2. **SAUTÉ** olive oil and garlic in a nonstick frying pan. When garlic softens, add a pinch of fresh mint.

3. **ADD** julienne sticks of zucchini into the frying pan and sauté on high for 2 minutes. Turn heat down to low and cover.

4. **HEAT** 1 tsp olive oil on high in another nonstick pan. Add garlic, a pinch of mint, and lemon juice. Add fish or vegetable broth and bring to a boil.

5. **ADD** peeled shrimp and cook on high for 2 minutes.

6. **ADD** 2 tablespoons additional broth around the edge of shrimp with remaining minced mint. Cover shrimp.

7. **PLATE** zucchini and shrimp. Drizzle a little extra virgin olive oil on top with cracked pepper, a dash of sea salt and a lemon wedge.

8. **SERVE** with a thin slice of toasted bread.

Mid-century Norman Cherner chairs, a custom live-edge table with a brushed stainless-steel base, and a stack of the client's Italian plates from Positano give this nook a sophisticated, European flair.

A blue and orange palette invigorates the otherwise neutral family room. I love the mix of patterns and colors—nothing is solid apart from the sofa. We layered in an abundance of textures, from embroidered and woven linens to touchable, plush strié velvet.

"THE BEST ROOMS HAVE SOMETHING TO SAY ABOUT THE PEOPLE WHO LIVE IN THEM."

— DAVID HICKS

IMMAGINE DI GIANCARLO GASPONI

ANDROMEDA DISCO

aperto ore 22.30

open 10.30 p.m

Via Cimatori, 13 - Firenze - ☎ 292002

VIVA ITALIA

When I give new clients my design questionnaire, two of the questions are, "What's your favorite place to travel?" and "What's your favorite hotel?" The answers give me clues on how to navigate style, design, and color. Often, the colors they like are in tune with the places they've been and hold dear. My clients honeymooned in Italy, and *la dolce vita* became part of the aesthetic narrative for the house, much to my delight. In 1993, I spent a semester studying art history in Florence and taking in the fabulous architecture, natural beauty, and of course, delicious food. These sensory memories influence my work to this day.

———

ITALY

Italy is one of those places I'll return to again and again. Life is lived in Technicolor here, and I take in the deep blues of the sea, the zingy yellow of lemons, and the attention to artisanship in the sculpture, ceramics, tiles and glass. From the old-meets-new streets of Rome to the sun-kissed colors of the Almalfi Coast, I find myself soaking it all in and refilling my glass with inspiration.

PERFECT PALETTES

Everywhere I go in Italy, I'm amazed by the vivid colors, but specifically the unexpected combinations. I'm always snapping photos of shutters, it seems, and my eye was drawn to how pale blue pairs so perfectly with terracotta and celery. Come to think of it, that palette has long been a muse for me—I painted this canvas (middle row, far right) as a student in Italy in 1993.

ROME

When in Rome, it's quite easy to get lost in the push and pull of modern fashion and design with the ages-old architecture that's everywhere. Whether you're sitting on a patio and eating the best pasta you've ever tasted or watching excited crowds make wishes at the Trevi fountain, the energy is undeniable. Nearby is one of my favorite buildings in the world; you can probably guess it's the Pantheon, for its magnificent domed ceiling with oculus. Rome has a stately, old-world elegance, too, which I experienced at a family wedding at the Villa Aurelia, where the flowers and overall setting were a sight to behold.

AMALFI COAST

Anticipation builds as you navigate the twists and turns of the Amalfi Coast and are rewarded with stunning views around every corner. Breathing in the salty air replenishes the soul, and the seaside towns are magical. Every experience is a feast for the senses. Le Sirenuse hotel in Positano boasts fabulous design and one of the best restaurants for a romantic, candlelit evening, La Sponda. But there's more to the picture-perfect Amalfi Coast than crystalline water and enchanting towns. Hike the Path of the Gods, which links various villages, to uncover a side of the coast that is still unknown to beachgoers. The winding clifftop trail is where you will have the most outstanding ocean view in the region.

CAPRI

The island of Capri is a special spot with many wonders to explore. The ancient Roman remains of Villa Jovis, built in 1 B.C., are well worth the 20-minute walk from Capri town. In addition to the ruins, there's a killer view—quite literally. It's where, according to legend, the mad emperor Tiberius used to push uninvited guests or disobedient servants over the cliff. You can also take a chairlift to the summit of Monte Solaro, the highest point on the island, and follow a trail map down past the hermitage of Cetrella. Here is a view of the famous Faraglioni, Capri's legendary trio of rocks that rise out of the sea. J.K. Place Capri is my go-to hotel and its interiors never fail to inspire. Don't miss dinner at Da Paolino, a courtyard surrounded by lemon trees near the main port, or Le Grotelle, in a location carved out of natural rock that serves legendary pizzas.

NEGRONI SBAGLIATO

Sweet, bitter, and refreshing.

1 ½ OZ	CAMPARI
½ OZ	APEROL
1 ½ OZ	MARTINIEROSSI VERMOUTH
3 OZ	PROSECCO
2 DASHES	ORANGE BITTERS
1	ORANGE

1. **COMBINE** all ingredients and serve over ice.

2. **CUT** coin of orange peel and remove white pulp. Light with match, quickly twist to release orange oils, and then rim glass and place in glass with cocktail.

Luscious orange-lacquered cabinetry and coordinating grass cloth walls and ceiling saturate the butler's pantry bar area, creating a cocoon-like feeling.

—

The solid brass custom console was inspired by the curvy silhouettes of the '70s—it asks for a piece of graphic floral art by Dan Baldwin. The embroidered drapery fabric is Les Rizieres by Les Ensembliers for Brunschwig & Fils.

—

Neutral walls and a white Bolon rug, a rubberized woven mat that looks like natural fiber, establish a clean ground to showcase the spool-style table that's lacquered in a deep marine blue-green, which resembles the color of the Mediterranean. Two-tone chairs in persimmon and royal blue velvet pull the room's energy toward the round table, where it becomes an intimate and festive gathering place for family and friends.

———

The dining table by French architect Jean Nouvel for Roche Bobois features a discreet built-in lazy Susan in the center, which is fantastic for entertaining. Handblown multicolored Murano glasses continue our Italian vibe.

———

Upstairs in the principal bedroom, the energy downshifts to calm and tranquil. It's a sanctuary. The custom bench—an homage to Berlin-born designer Karl Springer—boasts clean, tailored lines, and a bent waterfall edge.

————

Swivel club chairs in pairs are one of my signatures, and these are upholstered in a watery, painterly fabric that feels just right for the space.

————

I love to commission special handmade pieces that bring meaning to a room. These cross-stitched cushion shams were made by a women's cooperative in Jordan called Ayadeena, which translates to "our hands." Its goal is to improve the lives of skilled but underprivileged women, and their meticulous work adds to the room's sacred energy.

————

Not every table has to be created square or round. This custom, faceted piece was my way of thinking outside the usual coffee-table box and creating sculpture in the center of the room. It's a great shape for casual nibbles or family game nights.

OPEN-CONCEPT CHIC

Like me, these clients were not color-shy in the least. The living room overlooks a garden and pool and is open to the kitchen. Rich, luscious pinks, blues, and yellows feel both fun and charismatic enough for a young family with two children.

We had a wonderful opportunity to work alongside architect Christopher McCormack. We built out the bay window and trimmed it in walnut for a special touch. Then we mimicked its curve with rounded furniture. My canary yellow ostrich-leather mirrors add zest to an already lively scheme, and help to bounce light within the cozy fireside space.

———

The GP & J Baker linen, with its embroidered ribbons, isn't durable enough for the chair's seat, so I wrapped it around the sides and back. Its undulating pattern is complemented by the wavy brass side table.

———

Details take a kitchen from functional to memorable. Notching the stool backs into a V shape is an artistic move to trick the eye and draw it up to the architectural Gabriel Scott light fixtures, which also play upon unconventional shapes.

———

The push and pull of straight lines and angles is a source of fascination for me, and an area in which I'm always experimenting.

—AH

In the breakfast nook, a table base from Mr. Brown in London references
the iconic Saarinen table, but we took the reference in a new direction with
a back-painted glass top. The banquette's walnut structure is enhanced by
hex-topstitched leather and a Joshua Jensen-Nagle photo to pull it all together.

Energy comes from the element of mystery, a feeling that there's more than meets the eye. In this hallway, walnut panels with stainless-steel inserts create a grid pattern that conceals storage and a doorway into the home's office. A slight reveal in the paneling means there's no hardware necessary, which helps to complete the illusion. Gold feather sconces and a porthole mirror soften the abundance of hard lines.

———

The powder room goes psychedelic—this kaleidoscope wallpaper mimics agate geodes, which is a fun surprise for guests. We took the mirror across to the corners and up to the ceiling so the pattern wraps and repeats in infinite fashion; framing the mirror would have broken the spell.

———

A painting by the Canadian abstract painter Jack Bush sets the tone for this highly personal living space. A pair of art deco chairs purchased in San Francisco add a sculptural quality to the space and are complemented by the iridescence of the stone tabletop and a lime green sofa.

———

"ART IS AN ADVENTURE INTO THE UNKNOWN WORLD, WHICH CAN BE EXPLORED ONLY BY THOSE WILLING TO TAKE RISKS."

—

MARK ROTHKO

COZY

White walls and white oak herringbone flooring establish a fresh landscape. Walnut-trimmed doorframes give the main floor a warm yet modern feeling. The family's exquisite collection of Canadian art, and *Waterfront* by Momo Simic, inspired a palette of smoky grays and deep marine blues, loden green, ochre, and cognac in layers of leather, linen, wool, velvet, and felt.

COMFORTABLE, WELCOMING, SNUG: CURL-UP-AND-GET-COZY ROOMS ARE WHAT WE ALL CRAVE WHEN THE TEMPERATURE DIPS AND THE DARK DAYS LAST LONGER.

COZY AND CASUAL SPACES CELEBRATE THE SIMPLE PLEASURES WITH IMPECCABLE ATTENTION TO DETAIL. INSPIRED BY THE DANISH CONCEPT OF HYGGE, I LIGHT CANDLES EVERY NIGHT FOR OUR DINNER TABLE TO FOSTER A FEELING OF TOGETHERNESS AND RITUAL.

COZY STYLE IS A WARM EMBRACE FOR YOURSELF, YOUR FAMILY AND YOUR COMMUNITY."

EARTHY MODERN

The owners of this Victorian revival home, a sophisticated couple with three daughters, wanted pared-back spaces that would invite conversation and quality time. Working with our colleagues at Wayback Architects, we maintained the historic exterior and windows but took the interior down to the studs, rebuilding it with varied wood species and stones for a warmer, more urban take on Scandinavian style.

My client works in the mining industry, so we had a lot of fun visiting stone yards together to select unique slabs, including this unusual brown crackled stone for the living room coffee table.

———

A pair of sofas mirroring each other anchor the room and provide symmetry and ample seating for entertaining. We reframed the clients' art collection to switch from traditional, gilded frames to contemporary versions. Now, Claude Picher's painting above the sofa glows without distraction.

———

The Ella swivel chair by Niels Bendtsen is ergonomic and comfortable with its bucket dish shape, while simultaneously acting as a piece of sculpture.

———

SUNDAY MORNING

HOME AGAIN
MICHAEL KIWANUKA

I SAY A LITTLE PRAYER
ARETHA FRANKLIN

TUDO MUDA O TEMPO TODA
CELSO FONSECA, ANGALA

IF THE MOON TURNS GREEN
BILLIE HOLIDAY

QUIET NIGHTS OF QUIET STARS
STACEY KENT

WONDERFUL LIFE
KATIE MELUA

MISTY BLUE
DOROTHY MOORE

CAN'T HELP FALLING IN LOVE
KINA GRANNIS

SEPTEMBER MORN
NEIL DIAMOND

ONE OF THESE THINGS FIRST
NICK DRAKE

HARVEST MOON
NEIL YOUNG

HAWA DOLO
ALI FARKA TOURE

HAVE YOU EVER SEEN THE RAIN
WILLIE & PAULA NELSON

PRETTY STARS
BILL FRISELL

FEELS LIKE HOME
BONNIE RAITT

VINCENT
JAMES BLAKE

MY FAVORITE PICTURE OF YOU
GUY CLARKE

ALONE AGAIN
DIANA KRALL

**HOW CAN YOU MEND
A BROKEN HEART**
AL GREEN

LET'S FALL IN LOVE FOR THE NIGHT
FINNEAS

LESSON LEARNED
ALICIA KEYS

Black is so important to ground a room—especially one that's blessed with high ceilings and filled with light—and this bay window was the perfect spot for a grand piano, which frequently gets played!

A walnut dropped ceiling panel makes the entry feel compressed and welcoming. Like many heritage homes, this one did not have a hall closet near the front door, so we added a wall of closets around the corner in the dining room.

—

How do we make a room feel like a hug? Layer warm wood tones, carefully placed, strategic lighting, collected art, which brings meaning to a space, plush pillows, soft blankets, and a few casual handmade objects. These elements make us feel good and offer a sense of belonging. —AH

A solid walnut handrail with inset marble has visual and structural importance, embellished only by the sculptural Arrow pendant light by Apparatus Studio.

———

True luxury is captured by expert leather craftsmanship to create beautiful saddles at Hermès of Paris. The Belgian linen pillows trimmed with saddle-stitched leather reminded me of the artistry captured by the beautiful saddles at Hermès of Paris. The pillows add a subtle, refined detail atop the armchairs by Frigerio of Italy.

———

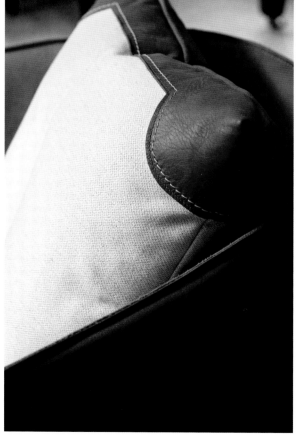

There's nothing like a round dining table to encourage conversation and intimacy. I designed this one with a faceted blackened nickel base to give it presence in the center of the room. The surface is made from honed Imperial Black marble with a reverse beveled edge. We couldn't find a dome fixture large enough, so we custom-made one; the gold leaf inside gleams beautifully at night.

In the dining room, a white oak buffet is stained a different tone from the floors to create subtle contrast. Its hardware-free design gives the piece a quiet modernity.

———

In a narrow space, a deep kitchen island isn't always possible. Inspired by Italian cafés where you down a quick espresso before heading out the door, we squeezed in a 25-inch-wide island and managed to house a steam oven inside as well as adequate storage. Wayback had the idea to face the pantry wall in walnut and wrap it across the ceiling to where an atrium shoots up to a skylight; the effect is cozy, chic and enveloping.

This family loves to gather for morning breakfast and rowdy card games after dinner, so we needed to create a comfortable, functional space at the opposite end of the kitchen. The couple often returns to London where they lived with their young family, and the inspiration for the banquet and bistro table came from their favorite cocktail bar at the Laslett Hotel in Notting Hill. A wall-mounted, diner-style bench is a fabulous solution for a narrow space. Here, I channeled just the back of the leather upholstery for effect. The hand-crafted Hiroshima chairs by Naoto Fukasawa appear to be carved from a singular piece of wood.

ANNE HEFFER 2003

ANNE'S CLAM CHOWDER

At the end of each summer, I take the kids clamming in Nantucket. I love to make a pot of steaming chowder—or "chowda," as we like to say—with a fresh green salad and glass of Chablis.

100	FRESH QUAHOG CLAMS*
6 SLICES	BACON
4 TBSP	UNSALTED BUTTER
2 TBSP	FINELY CHOPPED GARLIC
2 CUPS	DICED ONIONS
2 CUPS	DICED CELERY
2 TBSP	THYME, CHOPPED
6	BAY LEAVES
6 DASHES	TABASCO SAUCE
2 TBSP	WORCESTERSHIRE SAUCE
	GROUND PEPPER
½ CUP	FLOUR
2 POUNDS	RUSSET POTATOES, CUBED
2 CUPS	HEAVY CREAM
	CHIVES, FOR GARNISH
	OYSTER CRACKERS

If you choose to use frozen pre-shelled clams, buy 5 one-pound packages of baby clams. Thaw and strain clam juice, add the clams along with 4 additional cups of bottled clam juice to the pot.

1. ADD clams to stockpot, fill ¾ full with boiling water. Cover and cook over medium-high heat for 5 minutes.

2. DRAIN liquid through cheesecloth to remove any sediment, and reserve broth.

3. REMOVE clams from shells. Discard shells and chop clams.

4. FRY bacon in a large soup pot. Once bacon is crispy, remove bacon from pot, chop and set aside.

5. ADD unsalted butter to the bacon drippings and stir.

6. SAUTÉ garlic, onions, celery, and thyme, adding bay leaves, Tabasco sauce, Worcestershire sauce, and ground pepper.

7. ADD flour slowly and continue to cook until onions are soft but not brown.

8. ADD potatoes and clam broth. Cover and boil for 15 minutes.

9. REMOVE from heat and discard bay leaves.

10. STIR in clams and heavy cream.

11. GARNISH each serving with minced chives, chopped bacon, pepper, and oyster crackers.

The side tables feature a unique pairing of a waterfall-marble frame and leather-paneled drawers.

The couple purchased the Chinese wedding ceremony portrait during their travels in Asia. The intricate pattern of the Bamileke table, handmade in Cameroon, represents the web of the earth spider, a symbol of wisdom.

The original oak-paneled den, with its welcoming bouclé wool sofa, is where the family enjoys movie nights. Once again, contrasting wood tones keep the space feeling cozy but not too dark and intense.

On the upstairs landing outside
the bedrooms, a walnut-clad
nook offers a spot to read
or put on shoes. Storage is
concealed underneath
the bench.

A backlit mirror gives the main floor powder room a luxurious nightclub vibe.

———

The kitchen's marble wall carries up to a mezzanine containing the home office.

———

My husband and in-laws would call hygge 'Gemütlichkeit,' meaning cozy, warm, relaxed, and friendly in German—the feeling of family closeness at home. —AH

Smart technical moves, from a floating vanity with an integrated counter and sink to an LED-backlit mirror, make a complex ensuite look simple and serene. A rounded, freestanding tub infuses the room with organic softness.

———

In the soothing principal bedroom, the only color comes from the photograph by Wanda Koop. The white oak cabinetry in the his-and-her dressing rooms has a slightly different stain, just for fun.

———

A platform in the middle daughter's bedroom feels cool and loungy.

———

NEW ZEALAND

New Zealand is one of the few countries where I didn't spend time shopping. Our visit in 2013 was more about exploring the sensations of walking on an oceanside cliff, witnessing a Mãori tribal ceremony and dance, tasting fresh seafood, watching sheep graze, and sipping crisp, white wine. The scenery is beyond breathtaking.

WAIHEKE ISLAND
One of the most magical lunch spots I've ever encountered, hands down, is the perfectly manicured garden at Mudbrick. The sparkling views of the Hauraki Gulf, with Auckland in the background, are on par with the decadent farm- and ocean-fresh food.

ROTORUA
The middle part of the North Island is where *Lord of the Rings* was filmed. We spent a morning at Hobbiton, the movie set, where our kids frolicked around the hilly farm scattered with Hobbit Holes! Rotorua is also home to New Zealand's greatest geothermal wonders: there are many bubbling pools of mud, active volcanoes, geysers, and numerous hot springs to explore. We visited several Mãori tribe cultural sites and spent a wonderful evening seeing the cultural performance at the Mitai Mãori Village. We hopped aboard a charming old steam ferry to the Agrodome, where we learned about how New Zealand farms work. After taking in a sheep shearing demonstration, it struck me as remarkable to think about the origin of wool fabrics and textiles.

LAKE TAUPO
This area is a nature lover's paradise. Here, we experienced magnificent views of deep blue waters, snow-capped volcanic craters, craggy mountains, and pristine forests.

HAWKES BAY
Hawkes Bay is the Napa Valley of New Zealand, where eating and drinking well are serious local sports. The Farm at Cape Kidnappers is a small luxury resort in Hawkes Bay with a world-class golf course. It's a

phenomenally beautiful piece of land with rolling green hills, untouched forest, and dramatic cliffs that fall into the Pacific. The farmhouse lodge there made such an impression on me; its reclaimed wood and gray stonework, high-peaked ceilings, and beautiful windows made us want to rebuild our dream cottage back at home (and we did!). Don't miss the gannet colonies to spy rare and distinct birds. Also book ahead with a guide to view the endangered kiwi bird.

QUEENSTOWN
As much as I was able to relax and enjoy our downtime exploring this beautiful country, this is the one spot that spiked my blood pressure! Queenstown is the adventure capital of New Zealand and is home to high peaks, serene lakes, and just about any adrenaline activity you could ever hope to try. I guarantee that an extreme activity like bungee jumping, hang gliding, or jet boat racing through Shotover Canyon at 85 mph will take your mind off your day-to-day anxieties at home.

MILFORD SOUND
It's worth splurging on a helicopter excursion to Milford Bay and soaking up the most dramatic scenery in New Zealand. We landed on the glacier and stepped out onto the ice—wow, it was like being on another planet. After taking off again, we flew up the coast and landed on a deserted beach that looked bright and iridescent thanks to the iconic paua shells, also known as abalone. At the end of the journey, you'll understand why Rudyard Kipling once called Milford Sound "The Eighth Wonder of the World."

UNDERSTATED ELEGANCE

For this well-traveled family, we created warm, neutral spaces with comfortable furniture and mementos from their favorite trips abroad. Though most rooms in this home are creamy and bright—and not your typical definition of cozy—the layers and personality invite curling up and connecting with others.

Though the custom upholstery is tailored, the seats are loose and easy to sink into. The soft putty-colored walls add warmth along with a wool rug that has a subtle geometric knotted pattern. Two Carvers' Guild mirrors ground consoles from my *ah ha!* collection, and a painting by Erin Rothstein draws the eye to the fireplace. The inlaid penn shell and brass double-tiered cocktail table is by my friend Garrison Rousseau.

TOP 20 MOVIE NIGHT PICKS

1   OUT OF AFRICA

2   ROMAN HOLIDAY

3   SCENT OF A WOMAN

4   THE COLOR PURPLE

5   A ROOM WITH A VIEW

6   GOOD WILL HUNTING

7   NOTTING HILL

8   FRIDA

9   THE NOTEBOOK

10 TOP GUN

11 THE LAST EMPEROR

12 JULIE & JULIA

13 A STAR IS BORN

14 THE ROYAL TENENBAUMS

15 A RIVER RUNS THROUGH IT

16 THELMA & LOUISE

17 EAT, PRAY, LOVE

18 BRIDESMAIDS

19 LITTLE WOMEN 2019

20 THE TALENTED MR. RIPLEY

A Parsons-style shagreen console with upholstered cubes beneath is one of my favorite tricks for creating extra seating. The silhouette of the Chuck Close has strength in the airy space.

———

Touchable velvet brings instant coziness to a room. We chose two shades for the pillows—a mossy green and a chartreuse—to bring life into the house and foster a connection with nature.

———

The walnut-paneled study is full of personal items and memorabilia. Velvet once again plays a role—here on a timeless, rolled-arm sofa with nailhead trim. The papercut by artist Ed Pien creates a moment in the center of the millwork and gives the eye a place to pause. The chair, which my clients brought back from Budapest, Hungary, is upholstered in Scalamandré velvet.

———

Grass cloth wallpaper is forever. I'll never stop using it because it adds an organic layer that painted drywall can never provide. It elevates any space with its natural, handmade feel.

———

The Oly Studio pendant, which hangs above the round dining table by Netherlands designer Marlieke van Rossum, is made from cast resin. We chose cheery, apple-green Lorae chairs by Bright Chair for the breakfast nook to mirror the outdoor views.

——

WHITE BEAN CHICKEN CHILI

Family-style comfort food with Mexican flair.

1	ROTISSERIE CHICKEN
2	POBLANO PEPPERS
2 14 OZ. CANS	WHITE BEANS, DIVIDED
2 TBSP	OLIVE OIL, DIVIDED
4 CLOVES	GARLIC, MINCED
2 MEDIUM	YELLOW ONIONS, MINCED
½ TSP EACH	SEA SALT AND PEPPER
½ TSP	PAPRIKA
½ TSP	OREGANO
1 TSP	CHILI POWDER
1 TBSP	GROUND CUMIN
1 TBSP	GROUND CORIANDER
6 CUPS	LOW-SODIUM CHICKEN STOCK
3	LIMES, JUICED
3 CUPS	FROZEN CORN
½ CUP	HALF-AND-HALF CREAM

FOR GARNISH:
DOLLOP SOUR CREAM
SHREDDED MONTEREY JACK CHEESE
FRESH CILANTRO, CHOPPED
GREEN ONION, CHOPPED
JALAPEÑO PEPPER, CHOPPED
AVOCADO SLICES
SLIVERS OF TORTILLA CHIPS

1. HEAT oven to 425 degrees.

2. REMOVE skin and bone from rotisserie chicken, then shred meat.

3. COAT poblano peppers in 1 tbsp olive oil and roast until charred. Remove from oven, place in a heat-safe bowl and cover with plastic wrap. Wait 10 minutes, then remove stem, skin, and seeds.

4. DRAIN & RINSE 2 cans white beans.

5. PURÉE peppers and half of white beans.

6. HEAT 1 tbsp olive oil in Dutch oven over medium-high heat. Add garlic and onion, and sauté until soft and fragrant.

7. ADD sea salt, ground pepper, paprika, oregano, chili powder, cumin, and coriander. Sauté for 10 minutes.

8. STIR in white bean and pepper purée plus chicken broth and juice of 2 limes.

9. SIMMER for 30 minutes.

10. ADD remaining white beans, shredded chicken, and frozen corn.

11. COOK on medium heat for 10 minutes, until heated through.

12. TURN off heat and stir in cream. Serve in individual bowls and garnish as you wish.

TRUE BLUE

My client asked for an enveloping room and blue is her favorite color, so we went all the way with a deep, ocean-blue grass cloth wallpaper and lacquered trim. The combination of blue and white is classic, and the geometric print on the roman shades injects interest and movement.

Working with the shape of the rounded bay window, I created a curved-back custom template sofa to fit into the bay like a glove. The round motif continues in the ball pillows, rounded chairs, and Aoyama coffee table by Gubi, which features a stunning, nearly transparent laser-cut steel base.

Plush fabrics and brass accents add to the roc
warm, decadent mood. A playful photograph
Rodney Smith looks fresh above a white stone mar

This living room's geometric rug sets a glam stage for a tactile mix of polished metal and plush textiles. A painting by Harding Meyer creates eye contact that pulls you into the space, and then once seated, the room's lounge vibe invites you to mix a cocktail, put on your favorite tunes, and stay awhile.

———

SEXY STYLE TAKES ITS CUES FROM SUMPTUOUS FABRICS (THINK VELVETS, ANIMAL PRINTS, AND RICH BLACK ACCENTS) AND COME-HITHER FURNITURE. SEXY DOESN'T HAVE TO MEAN DARK AND MOODY. THESE ROOMS ENVELOP AND SEDUCE WITH THEIR INHERENT SOPHISTICATION—PERFECT FOR ENTERTAINING A CROWD OR JUST STAYING IN *À DEUX*."

BRING ON THE BLING

Joyful energy radiates from every room of this family home. Created for a cool young couple with two sons, it's both a respite from the hectic outside world and a place to welcome friends and family. The architecture is traditional with an interior envelope of crisp whites and grays, but the fixtures and furnishings we introduced are luxe, edgy, and fashion-forward—just what our clients craved.

An asymmetrical brass mirror and a blue Lucite console inject a little rock 'n' roll glamour to the entryway, elevating it above its traditional paneling and black and white marble floors.

———

We filled the curved space with a crisp, skirted table topped with black glass. A sculptural painting by Malcolm Rains completes the composition.

———

It's important to consider the ceiling and not just the walls. The antiqued mirror between the coffered ceiling panels and a hand-blown-glass Sputnik chandelier add sparkle and a reflective surprise.

———

Statement tables add a certain je ne sais quoi to every room, so I seize every opportunity. Here, the surface of a poured acrylic resin coffee table creates a 3D bubble pattern and plays off a blue ostrich-leather side table from my collection.

———

The dining room is formal and festive. I selected
a linear chandelier by Gabriel Scott, which adds
geometry, while a large-scale photograph by
Kristian Schuller called *Butterfly* draws the eye
in from the entryway. A black-and-white chevron-
patterned rug mimics the silver grass cloth walls.

When I think of sexy, I think of the words *drama* and *stage presence*. *Confident, alluring,* and *unpredictable* also come to mind. —AH

With gray and white as the backdrop, my yellow ostrich-leather desk adds a pop of lively color and makes a statement. The family room overlooks the loggia, pool, and garden. It's an open-concept kitchen, dining, and lounge room, and we pulled some of the pool blues into the space to bring in that outside energy.

———

The key to getting work done at home is having a beautiful office. We chose a warm-and-cool palette to bring together stately shades of gray with gleaming hits of brass. My favorite gray paint is Lamp Room by Farrow & Ball. A leather desk feels like the ultimate work-from-home indulgence and makes the hours pass by with pleasure.

———

"INNOVATION IS OFTEN THE ABILITY TO REACH INTO THE PAST AND BRING BACK WHAT IS GOOD, WHAT IS BEAUTIFUL, WHAT IS USEFUL, WHAT IS LASTING."

SISTER PARISH

Dramatic slabs of Statuario Venato marble provide subdued movement on the kitchen walls and allow youthful details—like the custom turquoise-and-polished-nickel pendants by the Urban Electric Company—to take the spotlight.

———

Circles and curved edges in the pendant, chairs, and table soften the linear detail of the room's coffered ceiling and make the space feel more approachable.

———

There's no shortage of seating in the open kitchen and living area, which includes an inviting reflective glass–topped round table with built-in lazy Susan.

———

A pair of custom swivel chairs upholstered in a turquoise-and-white geometric fabric by Jonathan Adler makes a natural transition from the sunroom to the shimmering pool beyond.

———

The backyard loggia is a magical, sophisticated adult playroom with its tailored white chairs, limestone floors, and black lanterns. This outdoor living room is an irresistible place to unwind, especially when surrounded by flickering candlelight on summer evenings.

———

Clear, crystalline turquoise
was the natural accent
for the sunroom and loggia
as a way of tying it all
together with the pool.

—AH

The rock crystal chandelier by Christopher Boots is an elegant piece of jewelry for an understated principal bedroom that's layered with touchable textures and tones of white, cream, gray, and smoky blues. —AH

A table lamp with stacked white, chamfered cubes is unexpected when paired with a gridded suede headboard and rectangular stainless-steel-framed mirror.

———

"SEX APPEAL IS 50 PERCENT WHAT YOU'VE GOT, AND 50 PERCENT WHAT PEOPLE THINK YOU'VE GOT."

—SOPHIA LOREN

NIGHT & DAY

There was much thought put into the intricacies and functionality of this new-build boathouse while incorporating earthy layers of global finds. I mimicked the black outline of the surrounding windows in the outline of the kitchen millwork for cohesiveness and contrast. Then I layered the space with crisp white pieces and warm wovens. The space feels like a true hideaway where you get lost in the breathtaking views and airy, eclectic vibes that beckon all day and all night.

We sewed together two vintage African Tuareg rugs to give us the larger scale we needed for the living space. Made from palm reeds and leather, these rugs are meticulously woven by hand. For practicality, the upholstery is covered in durable, stain-resistant indoor-outdoor fabrics. The stainless-steel coffee table base, which reflects the rug in its mirrored surface, adds shine and anchors the room.

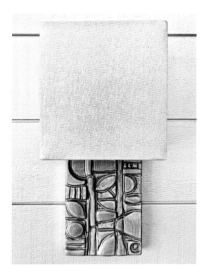

With its doors wide open, the boathouse offers a spot to put up your feet and exhale while taking in the 180-degree views of the lake. We considered windows and doors without the mullions, but I think the detail adds something special and is more interesting than plain glass sliders.

———

Layered lighting is key to the creation of a relaxed, sexy mood. Here, I introduced artisanal glazed ceramic wall sconces with a vintage vibe by Cedar & Moss, and of course, the massive woven pendant shade over the coffee table.

———

Natural beechwood caned
stools from Solos and a rope-
wrapped mirror behind the
sink are summer-fresh accents
that ground the proliferation
of white and black.

———

CHICKEN, PRESERVED LEMON & OLIVE BRIOUATS

This recipe comes from Tara Stevens and Rebecca Eve, who run the Courtyard Kitchen cooking school in Fez, Morocco. It's a very good way to use up leftover chicken, from a Sunday roast for example, and it's a fun canapé to serve with a glass of fizz. For me it is the taste of Fez: salty, spicy, savory, and sweet all in one perfect, crunchy bundle.

2 TBSP	BUTTER, DIVIDED
1 TBSP	OLIVE OIL
1 LARGE	ONION, THINLY SLICED INTO HALF-MOONS
3 CLOVES	GARLIC, THINLY SLICED
2	CHICKEN BREASTS
1 TSP	GROUND GINGER
1 TSP	SWEET PAPRIKA
1 TSP	TURMERIC
1 TSP	SAFFRON, CRUMBLED
½	PRESERVED LEMON, FLESH DISCARDED, AND PEEL WELL RINSED AND CUT INTO THIN STRIPS
4 ¼ OZ (120 G)	GREEN OLIVES, PITS REMOVED AND SLICED INTO ROUNDS
2 TBSP	FRESH CILANTRO
8 OZ (¼ KG)	PHYLLO DOUGH
1	EGG, BEATEN

1. PREHEAT oven to 350°F (180°C).

2. MELT 1 tbsp butter and olive oil together in a pan over low-medium heat, adding onion and garlic.

3. ADD chicken breasts, and cook until vegetables are soft and translucent and just starting to turn golden, and chicken is opaque. (It doesn't need to be completely cooked.)

4. REMOVE chicken and set aside. Add ginger, paprika, turmeric, and saffron to onion mixture and stir well to combine.

5. ADD preserved lemon peel and olives, and cook for about 10 minutes to let the flavors amalgamate. (Add a splash of water if it starts to look dry—this dish should be moist, but not wet.)

6. SHRED the cooled chicken with your fingers, then return to pan and combine well with other ingredients, stirring until chicken is cooked through.

7. REMOVE from heat, and stir in cilantro. Let cool.

8. CUT phyllo dough into squares to fold into triangles as you would with spanakopita, ensuring you allow enough to fold around meat mixture.

9. PLACE the filling in the center of the squares and top with fresh cilantro leaves.

10. BRUSH exposed sides of phyllo with reserved 1 tbsp butter, melted, to help seal packages, then wrap up in whatever shape you like. Brush tops of packages with beaten egg.

11. BAKE 10 to 15 minutes, until golden and crisp.

HARISSA-HONEY DIPPING SAUCE

30 ML	HARISSA PASTE
30 ML	HONEY (ADD MORE IF YOU PREFER A SWEETER SAUCE)
30 ML	ROSE WATER
30 ML	LEMON JUICE
1 TBSP	FRESH MINT, CHOPPED

1. COMBINE all the ingredients in small bowl.

2. CHECK for sweetness, heat, and acidity, adding more harissa, honey, and lemon juice as needed.

3. REST for 10 minutes before serving.

Every item chosen has a grounded, earthy, and handmade quality, from the hand-knitted pillow shams by Cotton Tree in South Africa to the airy David Trubridge pendant overhead and another Tuareg rug that feels beautiful underfoot. It's mesmerizing to lie in bed and watch the weather or seasons change outside.

———

The curves of a pill-shaped mirror, oval deck-mount vessel sink, and round pendant shade break up the linear wallboards and striped shower.

———

Contrasting arctic gray and white dolomite marble create stripes, which completes the shower and makes the design cohesive.

———

"YOU HAVE TO PUT YOUR FEET INTO YOUR DREAMS IF THEY'RE EVER GOING TO BE A REALITY."

– PAUL NEWMAN

The downstairs bar has a pass-through with retractable pocket windows for serving food and beverages—a fun solution for entertaining guests outside while you're prepping inside. Italian ceramic tiles by Mutina, floating walnut shelves, matching cabinet pulls, and LED lights with satin brass accents give this hardworking zone its sleek, Euro flair.

The boathouse is a haven for enjoying cold drinks, easy appetizers, and early dinners—and a place to retreat by the water's edge. —AH

Beneath the living space is an open-air cabana with a roof overhead to protect from sun and wind. Navy tones add a nautical mood, perfect for entertaining and "docktails."

MOROCCO

Morocco is exciting because it's full of contrasting sensory elements—mysterious, bustling, dusty city alleys give way to breathtaking vistas of desert, mountains, and sea. Earthy palettes reflected in the casbahs and Palmeraie oasis mix with the vibrant colors of tiled mosaics. The rich aromas of savory tagines (think saffron, cumin, turmeric, ginger, pepper, and coriander) are offset by amber and musk incense and the sweetness of rosewater. Talk about stimulating the senses! I was in awe of the crafts, such as ceramics, embroidered caftans, pom-poms, woven leather, embossed poufs, and babouche slippers. And then there are the Beni Ourain rugs and wood carvings inlaid with mother-of-pearl—I could go on and on.

———

"IN MOROCCO, I REALIZED THAT THE RANGE OF COLORS I USE WAS THAT OF THE ZELLIGES, ZOUACS, DJELLABAS AND CAFTANS. THE BOLDNESS SEEN SINCE THEN IN MY WORK, I OWE TO THIS COUNTRY, TO ITS FORCEFUL HARMONIES, TO ITS AUDACIOUS COMBINATIONS, TO THE FERVOR OF ITS CREATIVITY. THIS CULTURE BECAME MINE, BUT I WASN'T SATISFIED WITH ABSORBING IT; I TOOK, TRANSFORMED AND ADAPTED IT."

—

YVES SAINT LAURENT

A collection of trinkets, business cards, photos, and textiles from my last trip to this exciting country that's full of contrasting sensory elements.

———

MOROCCO

Morocco is a shopper's paradise, so be sure to bring an extra suitcase for your haul of treasures. If you've never strolled through a medina before, prepare yourself for the unexpected; it's sometimes raw, sometimes fragrant (good and bad), sometimes silent, and sometimes filled with the lively bartering of a salesman. Rich in culture and history, this is a place to lose yourself, to deepen your appreciation for handcraft, to taste many delicacies, to wander, admire, wonder, and feel the distant presence of the past.

FEZ

Welcome to one of the largest, urban pedestrian areas in the world! Fez is the cultural and religious heart of the country where the labyrinth of streets holds no end of surprises. Walking around narrow, winding, walled streets, you get the sense that you're in the middle of a massive maze, falling under its spell as you inevitably lose your way. Enter the nooks and crannies of the medina, where you'll learn about neighborhood bread ovens, see craftsmen at work, visit traditional schools, and meet many donkeys— the preferred method of transport. Hold your nose and open your eyes; you've never seen anything quite like this. Do enlist the services of a Moroccan henniya, a woman skilled in the art of henna tattooing, for an authentic experience.

CHEFCHAOUEN

Nestled deep in the Rif Mountains three hours north of Fez, this is one of the country's most picturesque villages, dappled in periwinkle blue. Its tiny medieval medina begs for photos at every turn, with dazzlingly blue whitewash and charming doors, alleyways, small shops, and crisp mountain air.

MARRAKECH

El Fenn, the riad where we stayed, is a jewel box of a hotel that beckons travelers with its glittering tile, and billowing curtains. There's so much to do and see, from the Majorelle Garden to the Ben Youssef Medersa and El Badi Palace. For shopping, hit the Quartier Industriel Sidi Ghanem in the morning, where a number of

high-end, design-focused stores have their showrooms and ateliers. Pass by Rue Majorelle, and plan for lunch at Grand Café de la Poste. If you're looking for relaxation, the spa at Royal Mansour is a must-visit, followed by dinner at La Grande Table Marocaine to take in the sumptuous surroundings.

MERZOUGA

A long but scenic drive from Fez across the beautiful and desolate Middle Atlas Mountains eventually takes you to one of the most spectacular and surreal vistas of the Sahara Desert. Visit the local souks in Rissani and try the sweet local dates; see salt traders, traditional blacksmiths, and the spice market. I bought some traditional Berber bracelets in a cool trinket shop. An hour and a half before sunset, head out into the dunes on camels to spend the night in a tent—and try not to think about a sandstorm coming through like it did when we were there!

SKOURA

From Merzouga, we drove to Skoura, the desert oasis where Dar Ahlam is located. If I were to splurge on one thing in life, it would be a stay at his hotel. I'm not going to say anything else because it would ruin the surprises.

ESSAOUIRA

Explore the old, exotic seaside town and shop the local galleries to the medina's tiny Jewish quarter. Here, you'll admire fishermen working their nets and hauling in the day's catch and snap some photos at the old port fortification. Head to the beach for lunch or get some kitesurfing lessons while witnessing Arabian horses trotting in the distance.

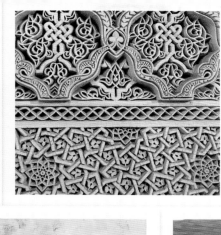

WELL TRAVELED

Travel has always influenced my design decisions. The scheme for this couple's home came to me in Marrakech, Morocco, while visiting the magical Majorelle Garden. The highly pigmented blue villa with canary-yellow accents popped against a gray, rainy sky—and inspired me to recreate that feeling in a transitional city home.

When the chairs steal the spotlight, a Lucite cocktail table feels like the perfect accompaniment: practical but visually invisible. Varying tones of blue add energy to the crisscross, ribbon-like print of the sofa pillows. A Calacatta marble slab table appears to float on a polished brass base, which reflects the geometric pattern of the area rug.

My clients love clean lines and symmetry, so I soothed their senses with matching swivel chairs and consoles, and a Barbara Steinman piece over the fireplace as a grounding element. With that foundation set, I introduced a pair of cobalt blue Mitchell Gold + Bob Williams chairs and balanced that color with cushions and a lamp on the opposite side of the room. Interior decorator Billy Baldwin believed that every room needs a little touch of brass and black, and it's so true.

Lucite-framed armchairs introduce a contemporary note in a paneled and buttoned-up home office. The cove in the bookcase showcases a painting by Susanna Heller, because offices should be both beautiful and functional.

———

A frosted globe chandelier by Apparatus Studio is an ethereal solution to this bay window dining area.

———

As much as I love a classic all-white kitchen, changing up the recipe with a few hits of yellow brings a smile every time you enter the room. My clients were a bit nervous when they saw the paint chips for the Urban Electric Company glass lanterns, but they trusted my vision. I think the light fixtures make the space.

———

The silver-gray Bolon rug is not only stain resistant, but also provides a clean canvas for the "Klein"-colored GUBI chairs, which surround a custom dining table with a multifaceted, polished gunmetal base. The Gabriel Scott chandelier is sculptural and elegant, and a perfect counterpoint to Hunt Slonem's whimsical butterfly painting.
———

I look at spaces like they're paintings.
I think, "How am I going to fill this canvas?"

—AH

Getting saturated yellow and blue right is a delicate dance. I reflect upon that gray day in Marrakech and the way the vivid color came alive against the stormy sky. I looked for a fresh canary yellow and rich blue tinged with turquoise to make these accents feel deliberate. A David Hicks rug, geometric-patterned pillows, and curtain-tape trim stimulate the eye, while *Grace Kelly*, by André Monet, stares back at us.

COLOR INSPIRATION

MOROCCO 2015

Every textile in the principal bedroom is soft and plush, from the wool drapes and rug to the channel-pleated suede headboard and facetted mohair ottoman.

———

Subtle layers of textured materials, including velvet, suede, and wool, add interest and a tactile element. Here, a smoked dark gray mirror with mother-of-pearl frame hangs above a custom French-blue-stained oak side table and smoked crystal lamps.

———

THE DARK SIDE

When my clients ask for drama, I'm not one to shy away—it's liberating to have someone say, "Just go for it!" In this luxe and layered living room, my empty-nest clients allowed me to indulge their passion for art, color, and entertaining.

The star of the living room is a fabulous antique Chinese black-lacquered screen not unlike the one in Coco Chanel's Paris apartment. Its depth and inherent glow called for emerald green and a stylized, runway-ready Scalamandré velvet tiger print that feels just as classic as it does edgy.

"NO ROOM CAN BE CALLED 'PERFECT' UNLESS IT HAS REAL COMFORT."

—

DOROTHY DRAPER

For this sultry den, I chose a deep aubergine for the wall lacquer and a rich grape velvet sofa studded with brass nailheads. The pale lavender David Hicks rug lightens the room, as does the fluffy Mongolian wool bench. Leopard velvet pillows and brass accents add the jewelry to the jewelry box.

To give this powder room a luxe sensuality, I proposed covering the walls in flocked black velvet wallpaper in a 3D print that resembles shirred balloon shades. An ornate French gilded mirror and Rococo ormolu sconces dial up the drama another notch.

In the formal dining room, a space meant for hosting a large family, movement meets stillness. The black-and-white agate-print wallpaper vibrates as Robert Longo's paintings capture bodies in suspended animation. Kelly green leather upholstery gives a preppy, modern twist to Louis XVI–style chairs, while a gilded mirror and crystal chandelier impart a sense of classic elegance.

———

A print by James Nares feels spontaneous and daring. I toured James's studio around the year 2000. Not only does he have a magnetic personality, but I was in awe of his creation: a suspension trapeze that allows him to float above his canvases to create the perfect flowing strokes with his handmade brush.

———

Leopard-print, Moroccan Beni Ourain rugs, cognac leather, rich velvets, a signature fragrance, and a cozy banquette in a dimly lit corner—these things top my list of sexy style moves. With black as the throughline and adding contrast, the stage is set for sumptuous, tactile fabrics and crisp linens. Created with intention, a sexy room is a confident room. But what's the sexiest thing of all? Having the confidence to be truly, authentically yourself.

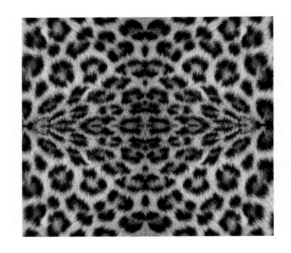

HIGH CONTRAST

There was plenty of charm in this old brick home but it was crying out for a face-lift.
I took my cues from my client's wardrobe—she always wears black and white.
The couple's photography collection needed white gallery walls, but my focus
was on using contrast and composition to create a first-floor entry lounge and
powder room that were as crisp and tailored as a tuxedo.

The placement of the original
fireplace was tricky, so to maximize
my clients' desire for another seating
area, my solution was two small
loveseats with polished stainless-
steel bases and velvet cushions.

The curved edges of a rectilinear bench mimic the rounded stair tread, while wrapping the base in brass pulls the eye up to the iconic disc pendant by Matthew McCormick.

Each piece exists as a unique element. We used shapes and an array of finishes, from polished metal to smoked glass, to give the room its super-sexy vibe. The curvy swivel chair introduces the only hint of pattern, and its tweedy texture reminds me of a classic Chanel jacket.

———

I'm often asked to make a powder room feel bigger than it really is. A massive mirror tricks the eye into thinking the marble porcelain slabs continue, creating a visual bookmatch effect. A black marble border on the floor, floating sink and toilet, and brass accents also give the tiny space a sense of grandeur and modernity.

———

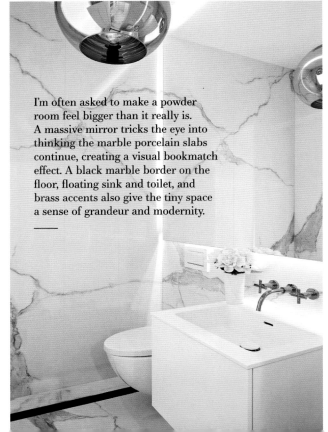

IN THE MOOD

STAND BY MY WOMAN
LENNY KRAVITZ

CAN'T TAKE MY EYES OFF OF YOU
LAURYN HILL

WILD HORSES
ALICIA KEYS FT. ADAM LEVINE

BLACK
PEARL JAM

KISS FROM A ROSE
SEAL

MISS YOU
ROLLING STONES

EVERYBODY HURTS
R.E.M.

LOVE ON TOP
BEYONCÉ

WICKED GAME
CHRIS ISAAK

SOMETHING TO BELIEVE IN
CITIZEN COPE

ALL I WANT IS YOU
U2

LOST TOGETHER
BLUE RODEO

SOMETHING JUST LIKE THIS
THE CHAINSMOKERS & COLDPLAY

HARVEST MOON
NEIL YOUNG

SO FAR AWAY
DIRE STRAITS

FOREVER
KISS

HOTEL CALIFORNIA
EAGLES

PURPLE RAIN
PRINCE AND THE REVOLUTION

BETTE DAVIS EYES
KIM CARNES

SULTANS OF SWING
DIRE STRAITS

SAN SAN ROCK
THIEVERY CORPORATION

TRANQUIL

WE ALL YEARN FOR A PEACEFUL PLACE TO ESCAPE, THINK, AND LISTEN TO SILENCE. THERE'S NOTHING MORE MEDITATIVE FOR ME THAN STUDYING LIGHT AND HOW IT SUBTLY MOVES THROUGH A SPACE; HOW COLORS BEHAVE AT DIFFERENT TIMES OF DAY; HOW SHADOWS CREATE THEIR OWN PATTERN PLAY. AS WE EXPERIENCE A MINDFULLY DESIGNED SPACE TO REST AND RELAX, "SERENITY NOW" BECOMES PART OF OUR DAILY EXISTENCE.

BAY VIEW LIGHTBOX

This was a special project: I worked with the late George Homsey, FAIA, a giant in the California modernist style, especially in the Bay Area. It was a great honor to collaborate with him, and I appreciated his attention to light, shadows, the planes of walls, and finding creative ways to puncture those planes.

When my clients purchased the building, I spent several days and nights studying the light. When the sun sets, there's a hint of haze in the sky and it creates a dusty, mauve-y purple that eventually gets deeper as night falls. My intention was to bring the evening sky inside by using soft, muted purple textiles, which create a soothing effect.

The console table was part of the legendary decorator Michael Taylor's collection and was purchased at auction in California; the standing lamps were a St. Tropez find. My clients and I both have an affinity for Buddha, so he's here as a welcoming talisman.

Because there are no windows in this small vestibule, I was interested in how we could achieve a natural iridescence. Rather than wrapping the walls, I framed two large panels in sparkly capiz-shell wallpaper. The walls are white but pick up a golden glow from the gilded ceiling light, a wall sculpture I found in the home department of Bergdorf's and transformed into a light fixture. It reminds me of a sunflower.

Two black-lacquered Hollywood Regency chairs by James Mont, upholstered in shimmery Fortuny, ground the grouping beneath a striking photograph by the late Brian McKee. It captures the way light punctures a centuries-old building in India, and it speaks to George Homsey's approach to this project.

The gallery light fixture and mirror over the fireplace are both by French designer Hervé van der Straeten. I love how they speak to one another in the open space. —AH

San Francisco gets chilly at night, so I focused on layers of warm, tactile fabrics.

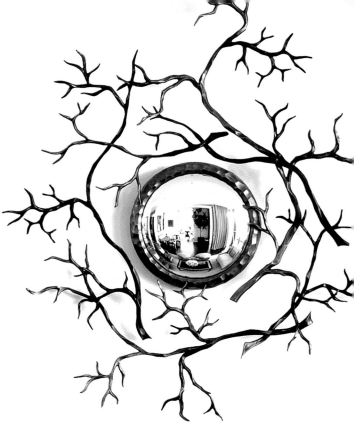

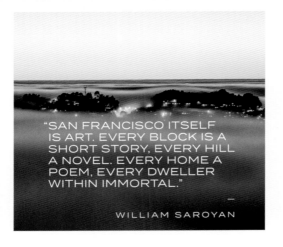

"SAN FRANCISCO ITSELF IS ART. EVERY BLOCK IS A SHORT STORY, EVERY HILL A NOVEL. EVERY HOME A POEM, EVERY DWELLER WITHIN IMMORTAL."

— WILLIAM SAROYAN

Dim Sum at Yank Sing

Telegraph Hill

Balboa Cafe

Architect George Homsey

Ferry Building

The dining room is intimate and expansive at once, with windows on both corner walls and stunning views of the Bay Bridge.

———

An interplay of circles and spheres makes this space unique, from the round walnut table by Hélène Aumont and round-back Klismos chairs to the gilded Niermann Weeks light fixture. We also applied beveled mirrors on the floor-to-ceiling china cabinet doors to reflect the views. Once seated in the space, it's hard to tell where the room ends and the sky begins.

———

"MEMORY IS THE DIARY WE ALL CARRY ABOUT WITH US."

OSCAR WILDE

Minty-hued upholstery on the banquette picks up on the backsplash tile and makes the breakfast nook feel light and fresh. The mid-century diner-style table is a favorite of mine; it's from Soane Britain. Green felt like the most appropriate accent for this kitchen. Though you can't see them here, a flock of green parrots are residents in the gardens below.

Sun streams down from a light shaft and illuminates the beveled Ming-green marble subway-tile backsplash, which goes all the way up to the ceiling skylight for maximum effect.

———

Ceiling-high built-ins frame the doorway to the kitchen and create a casual gallery of simple objects.

———

The kitchen island is situated beneath a spectacular round skylight, so a boomerang-shaped island becomes a sculptural feature grounding the center of the room.

——

CALMING CHIA PUDDING

As comforting as it is healthy.

1 CUP	CASHEWS
2 CUPS	COCONUT WATER
½ CUP	MAPLE SYRUP
1 TSP	CINNAMON
¼ TSP	NUTMEG
½ TSP	FRESH ORANGE JUICE
1 ½ TSPS	ORGANIC VANILLA EXTRACT
2 TSPS	HEMP HEARTS
½ CUP	CHIA SEEDS
1 CUP	FRESH BLUEBERRIES, STRAWBERRIES AND/OR RASPBERRIES FOR GARNISH AND BAKED COCONUT CHIPS

1. BLEND all ingredients except chia seeds in high-powered blender.

2. POUR blended mixture over chia seeds.

3. PLACE in refrigerator overnight.

4. SERVE for breakfast with fresh berries and coconut chips.

"KNOWLEDGE IS LEARNING SOMETHING EVERY DAY. WISDOM IS LETTING GO OF SOMETHING EVERY DAY."

—
ZEN PROVERB

Iconic Fortuny shams dress the bed while a button-tufted base with Lucite legs gives it a floating quality.

———

The principal suite's blue-gray palette is a moody and soft reflection of the sky and water view through the windows, especially on days when the fog rises through the bay. Custom shagreen panels add a luxe element to custom millwork framing the bed. Inside the shelves rests a treasured collection of Korean and Japanese porcelain, peppered with sea fans and organic beach material.

———

Sparkling glass and polished nickel add a slight art deco flair to the bathroom. Towels with embroidered chain links echo the key pattern on the dressing area doors.

———

A woman's dressing room is a sacred
place to reflect, primp, play, breathe,
and have time for herself.

I was captivated by the idea of creating flat-paneled, lacquered closet doors with a bold embellishment. The key pattern was digitally painted on to achieve precision. The polished nickel–framed door handles feature a leather inset.

———

Suspended silk and polished nickel pendants by the London lighting designer Hector Finch keep the surface of the cornflower-blue-lacquered linen dressing table clear and raise the eye up.

———

The packing table's chevron leather surface adds an earthy note. Here, the same Hector Finch pendant gets the oversized treatment, and its ruched periwinkle silk shade is a soft counterpart to the leather.

———

SRI LANKA

Sri Lanka, previously known as Ceylon, is a small teardrop-shaped island off the tip of India. We covered a large portion of the country in roughly three weeks, and its friendly people, breathtaking landscapes, vivid colors, and fragrant, spicy food remain in my dreams. On our active adventure there, we walked miles of beaches, we biked and hiked through ancient forts, cities, and rice patties, and we took a jeep through the dense green plains to see the Asian elephants in their natural habitat. Elephants are commonly depicted in art and temple carvings because they're considered spiritual animals. While touring around, we encountered iconography, shrines, and temples of all four religions (Buddhist, Hindu, Muslim, and Christian), reinforcing the island's serenity and calm.

THE CULTURAL TRIANGLE

In Sri Lanka's Cultural Triangle, which contains five UNESCO World Heritage sites, we spent three days captivated by 1,000-year-old ruins. Once a Buddhist monastery, Sigiriya was the royal capital of Sri Lanka for a few decades in the fifth century AD. After a great night's sleep at the Water Garden Sigiriya Hotel, we began our early morning hike up "Lion Rock," with giant paws. The same day, we hiked to the Dambulla Cave Temples, built in the first century BC, to experience the intricate paintings of Buddha and Deva covering every inch of the cave's walls. We explored the beautiful ruins of Polonnaruwa by bicycle and marveled at the massive stone sculptures of Buddha, both sitting and reclining.

COLOMBO

Colombo is the largest city in Sri Lanka, as well as its capital. The city is buzzing with cars, trucks, motorcycles, and tuk-tuks, yet urban life also has a sense of tranquility. I was awestruck by the walls and the ceiling paintings inside the Kelaniya Temple. Similarly striking is the city's oldest mosque, the red-and-white, candy-striped Jami Ul-Alfar. At the park Galle Face Green, we strolled with the locals while witnessing the new, modern urban developments next door. We stayed outside the city at the Wallawwa, an eighteenth-century country manor house converted into a small boutique hotel, which was the perfect quiet spot to recover after a busy day.

SOUTH COAST TO GALLE

The scenic coastal drive from Colombo to Galle has many fun stops along the way. We couldn't resist taking a break at Bentota, where our kids hopped on surfboards and took lessons for a day. We stayed at the Kumu Beach Hotel. A short drive away is Lunuganga where you can visit some of Geoffrey Bawa's structures. Bawa is the creator of the tropical modern style of architecture. We visited the Tsunami Photo Museum in Telwatta, a very sad and emotional exhibit displaying photos and messages from local people mourning the lives lost in the devastating tsunami that hit this area in 2004. We were also intrigued by the Kosgoda Turtle Conservation and Research Center, a nonprofit sanctuary to protect this endangered species. Rescued injured sea turtles are brought here for rehabilitation, and the organization conserves nesting sites and collects rescued eggs so that they can safely hatch. The young turtles are then released into the sea. At the Ambalangoda Mask Factory and Museum, we learned about this important part of Sri Lankan culture and history, before visiting Dudley Silva's Batik studio, where we observed the art of batik. On the southwest corner of Sri Lanka is Galle, a historic 300-year-old Dutch fort bordered by a sea wall; the colonial buildings make it feel like you've stepped back in time. At Barefoot, I purchased beautiful handicrafts, including handmade woven pillows from Kandy and the most divine incense.

ELLA & NUWARA ELIYA

We took an exhilarating train ride up through the magnificent countryside past the terraced tea hills to the charming town of Ella. We visited the Uva Halpewatte Tea Factory, the Ella Gap and Ravana Falls, and we climbed Little Adam's Peak. Our hike down to Nine Arch Bridge was timed perfectly to watch the train come through the mountain tunnel. The historic British colonial town Nuwara Eliya, near Lake Gregory, has charming vegetable markets and even a pink post office.

I was captivated by the variety of handmade textiles at Barefoot, where I purchased this intricately woven fabric from Kandy (left). This page features a Picasso-inspired piece from Dudley Silva Batik.

BEACH VIBES

A family getaway, this breezy retreat was a full renovation project.
The goal of understated elegance is achieved through use of organic,
textured materials upon a soothing landscape of white-on-white with
hints of blue to tie in the ocean views outside.

I've used bronze rain drums as tables in several of my projects and I love their unique
shape, patterns, and patina. These drums date as far back as 1,000 BC and are powerful
ritual objects used by the people of Burma and northern Thailand; when rained upon,
their sound is believed to please the spirits and attract more rain.

Natural meets '70s glam in the entryway, as a parchment console inspired by Jean-Michel Frank is adorned by vintage sconces with hanging glass panels. I bought the tribal necklaces in Victoria Falls, Zimbabwe. Abaca seagrass cubes are a great solution for extra seating when company comes over.
—

"I BELIEVE IN PLENTY OF OPTIMISM AND WHITE PAINT."

—

ELSIE DE WOLFE

The soft blue hues of the Blue Cielo marble backsplash and walls bring the crisp white cabinets into sharp relief and simultaneously add lapping wave-like movement.

———

In the living room, we introduced some deeper, solid marine blues and leafy printed indigo textiles to create contrast against fresh white. Wood elements add warmth via hand-carved Balinese teak mirrors and sconces fabricated from driftwood dipped in gold. These pieces all come together to give the room a touch of formality, yet the space is still inviting and calming.

———

The coffee table is my favorite part of this den—the base is a Balinese teak root, gnarled and beautiful, with a simple piece of floating glass to provide reflection without obscuring the sculptural quality of the root.

———

The guest bath's cerused oak vanity feels beachy yet warm, while suspended pendants interact with the mirror's sculptural shape.

———

In the guest room, a headboard upholstered in an indigo railroaded stripe spans the wall, so the two twin beds can be pushed together or pulled apart according to who's visiting. Wicker sconce shades and handwoven baskets from Zimbabwe give the wall above the headboard a textured, global infusion. In a classic blue-and-white palette, leopard shams, preppy stripes, Indian block prints, and a geometric patterned dhurrie rug are an unexpected mix.

———

Commissioned for the principal bedroom, the triptych above the bed is by Nantucket artist Peter Van Dingstee. Symmetry is so important in a bedroom suite, and pairs of everything—from lamps to tables and cubes—bring peace to the mind and eye.

—

An installation of 21 ceramic horseshoe crabs by artist Mark Rea makes the bathroom sing. I saw these in Nantucket and scooped them up because the color combo felt so reflective of the sea.

—

"IN ONE DROP OF WATER ARE FOUND ALL THE SECRETS OF ALL THE OCEANS."

—

KAHLIL GIBRAN

THE TRANQUIL TOP 20

Activities and objects, scents and flavors
that never fail to help me find my Zen.

1   YOGA AND MEDITATION

2   ROSEMARY AND LAVENDER

3   BATH SOAK WITH
    BUBBLES AND EPSON
    SALTS

4   BAKING BANANA BREAD

5   PUTTING ON A PAIR
    OF MY FAVORITE
    WORN JEANS

6   WATCHING A SUNRISE
    OR SUNSET

7   WALKING ON A BEACH

8   ARRANGING FRESH
    FLOWERS

9   SNUGGLING WITH
    MY DOG TESSA

10 VISITING A MUSEUM

11 TOM FORD NEROLI
    PORTOFINO PERFUME

12 STAN GETZ/GILBERTO
    ALBUM

13 HOMEMADE GINGER
    AND TURMERIC TEA

14 STUDYING A
    RARE ORCHID

15 IRONING TEA TOWELS

16 GETTING INTO A
    BED OF LUXURIOUS,
    CRISP LINENS

17 JO MALONE
    GRAPEFRUIT CANDLE

18 MESMERIZING FIRE

19 READING A BOOK
    IN SILENCE

20 PAINTING

Balapitiya Sri Lanka

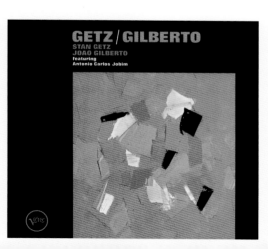

LAYERED LUXURY

This historic home belongs to an archaeologist, and when she's not buried in research or out on a dig, she craves a refined oasis that marries traditional and modern elements. Bold patterns and warm wood touches animate the neutral scheme with panache.

An icy yet soothing palette and plush silk carpet give the living room a dampened quality, like the silence outside after a heavy snow. Black accents add strength to the space, as do the important pieces of art by Brice Marden and Robert Rauschenberg. Front and center on the coffee table is a wonderful brass frog sculpture by Tony Duquette.

"MY GREATEST CONTRIBUTION HAS BEEN TO SHOW PEOPLE HOW TO USE BOLD COLOR MIXTURES, HOW TO USE PATTERNED CARPETS, HOW TO LIGHT ROOMS, AND HOW TO MIX OLD WITH NEW."

—
DAVID HICKS

A photograph by Edward Burtynsky hangs above a deep forest green parchment desk by Jean-Michel Frank, with a white chair upholstered in chocolate suede, designed by Garrison Rousseau.

Geometric patterns on rugs and pillows feel tranquil. Brushed-gold metals and rich, mossy greens give the oak-paneled den the sense of being inside a jewel box.

Taking a bath should feel like a mini vacation. —AH

One of my favorite solutions
is to add a barn door to avoid
a door swing in small spaces.
In this oversized bathroom,
nickel knobs on the vanity drawers
add the touch of polish needed
to elevate the space.

———

An inlaid palmwood bed makes
a striking statement in the principal
bedroom's creamy envelope. The
photograph over the bed is by
Christian Houge.

———

NOSTALGIC

MEMORIES GIVE DEPTH AND LAYER TO OUR HUMAN EXPERIENCE. THOUGHTS OF THE PAST BRING WITH THEM A SENSE OF HOME, COMMUNITY, AND CONNECTION TO WHAT'S MEANINGFUL.

I BELIEVE THAT WHEN WE GLANCE BACKWARD, IT HELPS US EXPRESS WHAT WE WANT TO SURROUND OURSELVES WITH IN THE NOW, AND THE FUTURE. FLASHBACKS TO SIMPLER TIMES GIVE US THE FREEDOM TO BE UNIQUE, AUTHENTIC, AND TRULY IN THE MOMENT.

Christian's Omi made this needlepoint and it's a precious keepsake. The fine handiwork and unapologetic colors make me smile whenever I see it.

___

A COLORFUL LIFE

Growing up in Greenwich, Connecticut, I had a wonderful childhood in the country, surrounded by my mother's beautiful cutting gardens. Inside, our home was bursting with bright, cheerful color and pattern, and I understood the power of home from a very early age. Our family enjoyed the perks of a 45-minute drive or train ride into New York City, experiencing all of the cultural activities the city has to offer.

Some of my most cherished memories are of my grandmother and namesake, Anne, picking up my brother, my cousins, and me in her big white Cadillac and touring us around Washington, D.C., where she and my grandfather lived. Anne, or "Gaga" as I called her, was a Southern belle and an artist herself. She would spend hours helping me decorate my dollhouse, making lampshades out of shampoo bottle caps, and teaching me about repurposed treasures. She was our tour guide, and she'd show us all the important historical monuments. I was always awestruck by the Washington Monument and the city's impressive architecture. I will never forget the one year we were lucky to attend the Easter Egg Hunt at the White House.

STUDENT

2 1207 00270 8465

PARSONS SCHOOL OF DESIGN
DEGREE CANDIDATE

VALID
SPRING 99

Morton, Anne C.
132552 AAS/InteriorDes

New School Univ

2000004192

Self-portrait
1990

Musée Carr

My Dad always said, "Do what you love to do most, and strive to be the best." That stayed with me. My first major milestone as a teenager was moving to Farmington, Connecticut, where I attended Miss Porter's School. There, I developed a passion for learning. Many teachers inspired me, including my advisor and English teacher, Rennie McQuilken; my art history teacher, Alice Delana; and my art teacher, Penny Prentice. These three people had a deep, long-term impact on helping me find my passions in life. It was there where I fell in love with art history and the fine arts. At Miss Porter's I learned a valuable lesson: I could do anything I set my mind to as a woman.

During my university summers at Vanderbilt, where I double majored in art history and human and organizational development, I studied or had an internship in many different cities in the US and Europe, where I gained independence being in new places. It was then I truly learned the value of hard work, but more importantly, how to work with people through being a good listener.

My first job after university was at an advertising agency in San Francisco as a junior account manager. I learned how to put together budgets and timelines for our clients, which is now such a key piece to managing residential projects today. During those years, I yearned to be on the creative side of advertising, so at night I took art direction and copywriting classes at the San Francisco Art Institute. In 1997, I decided to go back to school and study architecture and interior design. With my dad's voice ringing in my ear, I made a crucial pivot to find the creative passion I craved.

I went back to New York and attended Parsons School of Design. Finally, my future made sense and I found my calling. My summer studying in Paris was a deep dive for me into a love of design. After finishing school, I worked with Daniel Romualdez and soaked up his mentorship until, in 2003, I left his firm with the hope of starting a design studio of my own. I started my business, and Christian and I got married in 2003.

GARDEN FRESH

My clients' house has classical architecture, but the kitchen and family room were dark and dated. Though they are an active family with three boys, my clients are old souls who love more traditional things. I wanted to satisfy that craving while giving them a bright, vibrant space with a year-round connection to the beautiful garden just beyond the French doors.

A scalloped nailhead trim adds interest to a clean-lined navy sofa, while an array of tape trims mingle with solids and prints, making them feel like dressmaker details.

Add almost any bold color to navy and white, and you've got the formula for preppy style. In this case, apple green was a fresh and happy choice for a young family of five. —AH

TUNA POKÉ BOWL

This is what I crave when I want something crisp, filling, and healthy.

3 CUPS	WHITE SHORT-GRAIN RICE
½ CUP	SEASONED RICE VINEGAR
2 TBSPS	VEGETABLE OIL
¼ CUP	WHITE SUGAR
1 TSP	SALT
1 POUND	SUSHI-GRADE AHI TUNA, CUT INTO ½-INCH CUBES (WHILE STILL PARTIALLY FROZEN)
1 TBSP	SESAME OIL
3 TBSPS	LOW-SODIUM SOY SAUCE
1	LIME, JUICED
½ TSP	CHILI PASTE
1 ½ TSP	GINGER, MINCED

FOR TOPPINGS:
SHELLED EDAMAME
CHOPPED GREEN ONION AND CILANTRO
JULIENNED CARROTS, RADISHES, AND CUCUMBER
PICKLED GINGER
DICED MACADAMIA NUTS
SEAWEED SALAD
TOASTED SESAME SEEDS

1. **SOAK** rice in bowl of cold water, mixing occasionally. Rinse rice in colander until water runs clear. Drain for 30 minutes.

2. **COMBINE** rice and 3 cups water in medium-size pot. Cover and place over medium-high heat until rice boils for 2 minutes.

3. **REDUCE** heat to medium and cook for another 5 minutes. Turn off heat and let stand, covered, for 15 minutes.

4. **COMBINE** rice vinegar, vegetable oil, white sugar, and salt in small saucepan. Cook over medium heat until dissolved.

5. **COOL**, then stir into the cooked sushi rice. Let cool until rice is slightly warmer than room temperature.

6. **WHISK** sesame oil, soy sauce, lime juice, chili paste, and ginger. Pour marinade over cubed tuna. Mix and refrigerate for 1 hour.

7. **ASSEMBLE** bowls starting with rice, then adding tuna. Add toppings of choice and sprinkle with sesame seeds.

Though the luxe, all-white kitchen is serene, there's movement and energy coming from the coral-back chairs, scalloped periwinkle lantern, and fretwork on the upper cabinets, which complements the swoop in the transom above the French doors.

———

Faux crocodile upholstery is chic to look at and easy to clean after a family meal. Lantern is by Colleen & Company.

———

I used the same fabric for all the drapery in the open kitchen and family room. The print is called *Arbre de Matisse* by Quadrille and its invigorating color and pattern bring the outdoors in year-round; navy grosgrain ribbon adds preppy panache.

MIAMI PLAYHOUSE

The guesthouse at this Spanish-style villa overlooking Biscayne Bay was already a dream project—and then I found out about its musical pedigree. Ricky Martin, the home's previous owner, had used the building as his private recording studio. The 750-square-foot space had to be transformed into a guesthouse, but because it wasn't a primary home, my clients gave me free reign to realize my vision of a bubblegum pink and Kelly green palette inspired by preppy icon Lily Pulitzer.

Lily Pulitzer

The seashell mirror and console were special finds that brought the beach right inside the guesthouse—I call it "whimsical Florida chic." A green Buddha gives the vignette an unexpected twist.

———

I added a tape trim with wooden tassels at the base of the pink linen swivel chairs—when you turn in the chair, the lacquered green tassels sway like a flapper's dress.

———

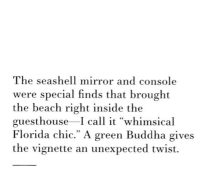

"LIFE IS A GREAT BIG CANVAS; THROW ALL THE PAINT YOU CAN ON IT."

— DANNY KAYE

The stepped headboard is upholstered in a Christopher Farr palm-frond print with art deco flair. I felt lucky to find the bamboo side table at auction and knew it was the perfect accompaniment to this tropical room.

————

I kept the bathroom simple, with shuttered vanity doors for a beachy vibe and pink, candy-striped shades on a pair of pineapple sconces for a touch of whimsy.

————

A scalloped pink lantern by Colleen & Company draws the eye up to the ceiling and balances out the solid pink rug. Matching palm-leaf-print drapes and headboard give this space full tropical impact.

————

"ALWAYS DESIGN A
THING BY CONSIDERING
IT IN ITS NEXT LARGER
CONTEXT—A CHAIR IN
A ROOM, A ROOM IN
A HOUSE, A HOUSE
IN AN ENVIRONMENT,
AN ENVIRONMENT
IN A CITY PLAN."

—

EERO SAARINEN

RETRO REWIND

The late '70s and '80s had a huge impact on my style, and these throwback icons continue to inspire and inform my designs today, from bubblegum colors and courtside preppy chic to impeccable tastemakers and playful prints.

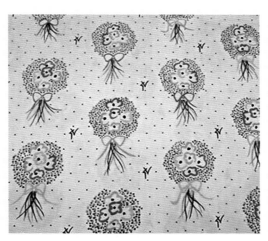

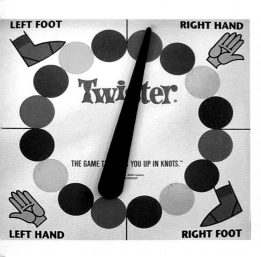

ISLAND TIME

This beautiful old historic building is nestled on 2,300 feet of island shoreline. My clients spent years painstakingly restoring the nineteenth-century home, and my mandate, once I arrived on the scene, was to fill the rooms with vibrant hues. The timing was perfect: I'd just come back from three weeks in India, so the colors and hand-blocked fabrics I learned about there were my guiding principle. These people are fun, eclectic, and even a little outrageous; they move up here for the summer and their cottage hums with kids, cats, and dogs. Their favorite colors are green and raspberry, so that became the jumping-off point for the preppy-boho getaway of their dreams.

Acid-green aluminum chairs from Janus et Cie call to mind the tree branches that surround the covered veranda—a favorite spot for alfresco family dining.

———

The cottage's front porch beckons with an assortment of vintage wicker furniture and aqua and lime Quadrille fabrics.

——

VODKA SOUTHSIDE

A classic country club refresher, this cocktail is usually made with gin, but I like the clean nature of vodka.

2 OUNCES
VODKA

1 ½ TBSPS
SIMPLE SYRUP
(USE CANE SUGAR)

3 DROPS
ANGOSTURA BITTERS

6
FRESH MINT LEAVES

1
LIME, JUICED

2–3 OUNCES
SODA

1. **MIX** vodka, syrup, bitters, mint, and lime juice in cocktail shaker with ice.

2. **STRAIN** and top with soda to taste.

"THE HOME SHOULD BE THE TREASURE CHEST OF LIVING."

LE CORBUSIER

We had fun with the smaller-scale seating area at the other end of the living room by repurposing wicker chairs and a loveseat—some painted, some left natural. Many of these came from the classic wooden boats, or "woodys," so prevalent on the area's lakes.

A blue-lacquered campaign desk has vintage charm when combined with cheery Nisiotiko fabric from Brunschwig & Fils and an apple green desk chair.

Here in the living room, we paired acid green and raspberry once again. Ceiling-high drapes soften the lines of the basswood tongue-and-groove paneling and add freshness. A glass-topped woven abaca coffee table by Ralph Lauren is a modern addition to a seating area with retro flair.

———

These old cottages were built to maximize the view. Big sky, big sunsets—it's all about nature. —AH

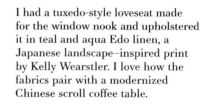

"DECORATING IS
NOT A LOOK, IT'S
A POINT OF VIEW."

I had a tuxedo-style loveseat made
for the window nook and upholstered
it in teal and aqua Edo linen, a
Japanese landscape–inspired print
by Kelly Wearstler. I love how the
fabrics pair with a modernized
Chinese scroll coffee table.

To help define the abundance of
space in the principal bedroom, we
built a dividing wall to make the
floating area around the bed feel
more intimate. Both the wall and
bed skirt are upholstered in a playful
Lulu DK bird print in lake-inspired
shades of blue.

INDIA

India was at the top of my bucket list for many years, so our trip there in 2013 was one of the most memorable and impactful experiences of my life. It was a feast for the senses, from the sunsets and colorful, embroidered saris to the fragrances of curries and street food, and the cacophony of horns blaring on the bustling streets. I had moments of joy when interacting with curious children, and moments of sadness experiencing the raw reality of poverty. The historic palaces and hotels throughout Rajasthan were an interior designer's dream come true, with intricate detail, vibrant colors, and mathematical, intricate geometric patterns that today would be considered modern—but they are in fact hundreds of years old. I also gained a deeper appreciation of craft as we visited many artists' studios to watch semiprecious stones being inlaid, marble carved, and silk textiles and dhurrie rugs woven. At a block-printing factory, I tried the technique, and it's not as easy as it looks! Indian inspired me, and is forever in my heart.

VARANASI

Our trip began in Varanasi, one of the oldest living cities in the world and the most spiritual Hindu site of India. We woke up before sunrise to float in a small rowboat along the sacred edge of the Ganges to witness hundreds of pilgrims cleansing in the holy waters. This ritual absolves the believers of their sins. It is the aspiration of every devout Hindu when they die, to be cremated at the ghats, the stepped riverbank, thus ensuring release from the cycle of rebirth. In the afternoon, we entered a decrepit building into a silk factory, where dusty antique looms were humming the creations of skilled weavers.

DELHI

Delhi is an intriguing mix of orderly, British colonial planning and quintessential Indian monuments. After a visit to Jama Masjid, the great mosque of Old Delhi (India's largest mosque), my friend Liz and I took a rickshaw down the crooked streets of Chandni Chowk, Old Delhi's colorful shopping bazaar. Within a busy day, we also saw the Raj Ghat, a memorial to Mahatma Gandhi, Nehru's House & Library, Ghandi's home (and site of his execution), the Lotus Temple, and the Crafts Museum.

AGRA

We arrived at the Taj Mahal just in time to watch the sun rise. The monumental building took 22 years and over 20,000 artisans to build, and appears perfect at every angle from afar, glowing in shades of amber. Close up, you can see the play between the patterned marble screens and their twin shadows on the walls and floors as the sunlight shines through. I was in awe of the semiprecious stones (mother-of-pearl, jade, malachite, carnelian, lapis lazuli, agate, and garnet) inlaid in the white marble walls depicting dancing flowers and climbing vines. The building is a love letter from Mughal Emperor Shah Jahan to his third and favorite wife, Mumtaz Mahal, who died after giving birth to their thirteenth child. Another noteworthy destination is the Agra Fort, built in 1565 by Akbar. The red sandstone citadel consists of palaces, courtyards, and terraced pavilions. Agra's old quarter, home to some of the city's best-preserved colonial architecture, is a legacy of the British influence that converted Agra into the industrial city it is today. From the railway station, we crossed over to the gigantic Jama Masjid, Shah Jehan's pearl-white marble imperial mosque, which was designed to house 10,000 worshipers.

JAIPUR

They say that when driving in India, you need three very important things: a good horn, good brakes, and good luck! We drove five hours from Delhi to the famed "Pink City" and capital of Rajasthan through cars, trucks, buses packed with people, motorcycles weaving in and out, as well as the occasional sacred cow in the middle of the street causing a traffic jam (plug your ears)! In Indian tradition, pink is the color of hospitality, and Jaipur fulfills this legacy both aesthetically and in spirit. Most structures are built using the area's indigenous dusty-rose sandstone, while others are painted pink. The Amber Fort, built high atop a hillside overlooking Maota Lake, was the early seat of the Amber kings. We strolled through the gardens, halls of public and private audience, and a labyrinth of hallways and passages leading to the royal apartments. My personal favorite was the Sheesh Mahal (Mirror Palace) where the walls and ceiling have intricately patterned designs in plaster with inset mirrors.

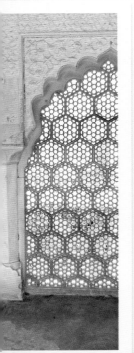

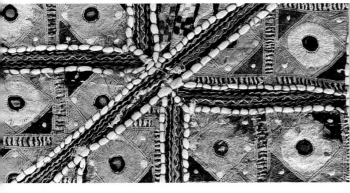

Apparently if someone lights two candles at night, the reflection converts into thousands of stars. We couldn't miss the Anokhi Museum, which documents the ancient tradition of hand-block printing. In Jaipur's City Palace, we experienced the Hawa Mahal (Palace of Winds), an extension of the zenana (women's quarters), where royal ladies observed the city's outside life in strict concealment.

UDAIPUR

Udaipur, the "City of Lakes," is one of the most picturesque cities in India, surrounded by the Araveli Range. Our most romantic hour here was spent on a sunset cruise on Lake Piccola, boating by the Lake Palace Hotel where James Bond's *Octopussy* was filmed in 1983, and seeing the twinkling city lights in the distance. The City Palace features stern Rajput military architecture on the outside, and over-the-top, Mughal-inspired decorative art on the inside. Walking through this mind-boggling maze of royal spaces, I was awestruck by the intricate, highly skilled craftsmanship displaying compositions of colorful lattice work, mirrors, and stained glass, and blue-and-white Dutch Delft tiles as well as mural paintings in relief. The palace museum houses a collection of intricate miniature paintings depicting scenes from the lives of the maharajas. In Udaipur's bazaars, I bargained for miniature paintings, wood carvings, silver, bangles, handmade notecards and more!

JODHPUR

The "Blue City" of Jodhpur, situated on the edge of the Thar Desert, echoes tales of antiquity. I highly recommend staying at the opulent Umaid Bhawan Palace, now a hotel, which is still the current residence of Jodhpur's royal family. It's furnished with the most sophisticated art deco furniture, rugs, and lighting! The impregnable and majestic Mehrangarh Fort was built by Rao Jodha in the mid-fifteenth century, when the city of Jodhpur was founded as the capital of the Marwar kingdom. Built on a rocky hill 400 feet above the city, it has a labyrinth of palatial buildings built by a succession of Marwar rulers. From the fort's ramparts there is an exceptional view of the periwinkle blue–painted Brahmin houses below.

ENGLISH LESSONS

This charming brick Georgian house belongs to clients who love traditional English decorating. My challenge was to deliver an elevated yet livable home with modern surprises to bring the interiors into the present.

I love using modern art to make a traditional space feel current. The photograph above the sofa is by Chinese performance photographer Liu Bolin, who earned the nickname "The Invisible Man" because he immerses and hides himself in his environments.

___

The living room's serenity comes from its tone-on-tone pistachio palette, with different prints and textures to keep it interesting to the eye.

———

Black-and-white checkerboard floors and black-lacquered doors lay the foundation for a timeless entry. A modern pendant and blue mirror layer in some contemporary edge.

————

The chandelier is a sentimental piece: my clients bought it on their honeymoon in England. I picked up on its classicism with a Regency-style mahogany table and shield-back chairs but added some unexpected elements like the greyhound photographs and Tibet Dragon-Tiger drapery fabric by Clarence House. I love that it's stately without being too serious and has a gentle nod to the '80s.

————

MEMORIES AND MAGIC

A CASE OF YOU
JONI MITCHELL

THE WAY YOU LOOK TONIGHT
FRANK SINATRA

I COULD WRITE A BOOK
HARRY CONNICK JR.

GREASE
FRANKIE VALLI

HEY JUDE
THE BEATLES

WILD WORLD
CAT STEVENS

KIND & GENEROUS
NATALIE MERCHANT

SATURDAY IN THE PARK
CHICAGO

I HAVE A DREAM
ABBA

I'M GONNA BE (500 MILES)
THE PROCLAIMERS

HOLIDAY
MADONNA

GIVE A LITTLE BIT
SUPERTRAMP

GALILEO
INDIGO GIRLS

VIENNA
BILLY JOEL

TOGETHER AGAIN
JANET JACKSON

JENNY FROM THE BLOCK
JENNIFER LOPEZ

DON'T PANIC
COLD PLAY

TINY DANCER
ELTON JOHN

MEMORIES
MAROON 5

I WON'T GIVE UP
JASON MRAZ

SOMEWHERE OVER THE RAINBOW
ISRAEL KAMAKAWIWO'OLE

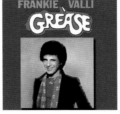

THE BIG PICTURE

When I step back and view life with a broader perspective, I'm keenly aware that design is about people. That awareness starts with my beloved immediate family and friends and extends to my wonderful clients. I'm grateful to have a chosen career that affects families' lives—including my own—day to day: the private spaces they wake up in, cook in, entertain in, and go to sleep in are sacred and removed from the outside world. It's an honor to be part of that process, and I don't ever take that for granted.

"EVERY TIME I PUT MY ARM AROUND YOU, I FELT THAT I WAS HOME."

— ERNEST HEMINGWAY

A year after marrying in 2003, Christian and I moved to Canada, where he was from, for our next chapter. My business as a designer and entrepreneur began to pick up, and then life got much busier and more exciting when we welcomed Jack and Charlie, our first set of twins. Three-and-a-half years later, I gave birth to our second set of twins, Amelia and Alexander. My kids have taught me that the joy in the little moments are treasures to keep. I'm always in awe of their words.

My daughter, Amelia, wrote this poem when she was in the fourth grade. The first time I read it, I thought, "She gets it." It's not easy to teach your kids; they are who they are. But seeing their depth is an amazing thing.

LOOKING FOR A NEW WORLD

Deep in the earth
A new song sings
Awaking seeds of
the coming spring.

Voice of the past,
voice of the land
which calls to remind
you on shoulders of
generations we stand.

The past is the stone
on which future depends
which uploads and heals
nature and defense.

Honor the land, the
power in you
Remember these words
to your own self be true.

—

AMELIA HEPFER

GRATI

Acknowledgments

To my parents, Kay & Bill Morton, for your encouragement and unconditional love and advice since birth! Thank you for giving me so many incredible opportunities during my youth. Thank you exposing me to art, culture, and style.

To my in-laws, Dorit & Wip Hepfer, you inspire me on so many levels to be free, present, and happy. I treasure all of our family time together.

To my brother, Will Morton. I love you, Avery and Graham. "Listen to the river sing sweet songs to rock my soul." —The Grateful Dead

To each and every client, thank you for your trust, for inspiring me, and for giving me the opportunity to create for you. Thank you for permitting me to photograph your home. Designing for your family is a great honor and brings meaning and purpose to my life.

To my editor, Beth Hitchcock, and art director, Rose Pereira: I couldn't have picked a better Dream Team for this project, and I've truly enjoyed each step of the process with you both! Thank you for your magic touches, for your passion and creativity.

To my talented team at Anne Hepfer Designs: Marina Abate, Paul McCluskey, Maloree Levine, Jody Nielsen, Jacquie Bernat, Tatjana Dimitrijevic, Marlie Cooper, Kelly Augusto, Greg Melong, and to our past employees who have contributed so much over the years. Thank you for all of your hard work, passion, and dedication to our clients and for seeing our projects through from conception to completion.

Special thanks to Gary Searle and to Doug Turshen for believing in me and my book project. Thank you for your invaluable advice and for your time!

To my publicist, Laura Bindloss, and the amazing Nylon team for working so hard to get our brand noticed.

To my editor, Madge Baird, and the Gibbs Smith publishing family for being the perfect match to get my book out there.

To all of the architects, builders, contractors, workrooms, craftspeople, suppliers, and trades, you have been our important partners in many years of passionate hard work. Thank you for supporting our team and clients, and for nurturing the success of Anne Hepfer Designs.

To all of the photographers who have captured many magical moments. Thank you so much for your artful eye. Don Freeman, you are so talented and it's been a privilege to know you and work with you.

To Kirsten Gauthier: from the beginning, you understood me and my vision to help define our brand.

Thank you to my extended family and very dear friends. I am full of love, deep respect, adoration, and admiration for each one of you.

TUDE

To the many people who have helped me along my journey and
have been instrumental in the development of my career and my life.
I am indebted to you all.

Allison & Matt Abbott
Karen & Marc Adler
Peter Allerton
Susan Arnold
Randall Atcheson
Danielle Baran & Glen Lexovsky
Alexandra Babcock & Todd Cowan
Nancy & Geoff Belsher
Lyndsay Bensen
Fred Bergman
Jack Bernstein
Cheyne & Mike Beys
Jennifer & Ugo Bizzarri
Fiona & Jamie Blair
Alison Booth & Jeff Campbell
Cally Bowen
Beth & Jamie Boyden
Kim Bozak
Beth Braithwaite
Sarah & Campbell Brown
George Bunnah
Cristina Burgess & Pat McCarthy
Susan Burke
Jim Burns
Nenita Calumay
Billy Ceglia
Christie & Fraser Chapman
Stephanie & Paul Coffey
Suzanne & Mark Cohon
Christy & Gord Cook
Terrance Deal
Cathy DeFrancesco
Carrie & Michael Degroote
Alice DeLana
Catherine & Bob Deluce
Justine Deluce & Dave Wiley
Laila & Michael Deluce
Alexandra & Brad Demong
Mandy & Jordan Dermer
Design Leadership Network
Michelle Doig & Jamie Biggar
Sophie Donelson
Brian Donovan, Paul Smith & Kravet
Heather & Michael Faralla
Martha & Geoff Fell
Cynthia Ferguson
Ken Dayan Flowers
Allison & Dave Fortier
Mike Fuller
Liz Gallery & Matt Tedford
Mary Gulizia
J. Gibson
Cheryl & Don Giffin
Dr. Bernie Gosevitz
Jane Halverson & Bruno Venditelli
Steph Nerlich & Chris Hardy
Alison & Jim Harris
Melinda & Tom Hassen
Stephanie Hill
Jen & Chris Hind
Sara Hirsch
Kelly Holinshead
Lisa Hough
The Kravet Family
Trinity Jackman
Brian Joffe
Denys Jones & Creative Custom
Chantal Kenny
Vered Klein
Neha Kotak
Caroline & Andrew Lapham
Arlette Tygesen & Michael Latimer
Cristin & Adam Lazier

Andrea Lenczner & Blair Levinsky
Patrice Lombardi
Jessica Everhart Ludvik & Kate Verner
Assoc.
Julia Malloy
Marisa Marcantonio
Cathy Martin & Steven Pauwels
Alex & Josh McCall
Heather & John McCallum
Janet & Peter McCarthy
Victoria McCowan
Adam & Katherine McDonald
Andrea & Mark McQueen
Rennie McQuilkin
Philip Mitchell & Mark Naransky
Muffy & Don Miller
Leo Mowry
David Murphy
Gina Navarro
Caroline & Chris Newall
Tripler Pell & Tawfik Hammoud
Courteney & Brian O'Hea
Richard Ouelette & Maxime Vandal
Joe Quinn
Sharon Polan & Bob Thornton
Sacha & Jonathan Pollack
Michelle & Robert Pollock
Leslie & Frank Pottow
Penny Prentice
Olive Purificacion
Joe Quinn
Zo Ratansi
Lynda Reeves
Heather Regent
Amanda Reynal
Sarah Richardson & Alexander Younger
Laurie & Dave Robinson
Danielle Rollins
Kenneth Roman
Daniel Romualdez
Eva Salem & Patrick Kedwell
Joanna Saltz
Robyn & Steven Scott
Gary Searle
Clare Sellers
Jackie Shawn
Johanna & Graham Simmonds
Sandy Skotnicki
Paul Smith
Christie Smythe & Christian Mathieu
Tommy Smythe
Doretta Sperduto
Laura Stein
Kelly & Alan Steremberg
Stephanie & Blair Tamblyn
Olga & Sergei Tchetvertnykh
Jeff Temporale
Teresa Track & Patrick Fejer
Jason Van Tassel
Tricia & Martin Vulliez
Kate & Dave Wallace
Alexandra & Glen Walter
Guan Wang
Victoria Webster
Martha & Sam Weeman
Sarah & Mark Wellings
Jennifer & Chris Willmot
Bruce Wilson & Primavera
Jordan Winters, Suzi MacDonald
Ali Yaphe
Leslie Zemla
Denise Zidel

PHOTOGRAPHY

To my dear friend and photographer extraordinaire Virginia Macdonald. Thank you from the bottom of my heart for putting your all into every shoot and for making my work shine. I'm so grateful to have you on the other side of the camera lens, and what a ride it's been—with lots of giggles along the way! — AH

PLAYLIST CREDITS

DANCE PARTY — 18

"You Are the Best Thing," **Ray Lamontagne**, *Gossip in the Grain*, RCA Records.

"Groove is in The Heart," **Deee-Lite**, *World Clique*, Elektra.

"Get Up Offa That Thing," **James Brown**, *Get Up Offa That Thing*, Universal Music Group.

"Don't Stop," **Fleetwood Mac**, *Rumours*, Warner Music Group.

"Gettin' Jiggy Wit-It," **Will Smith**, *Big Willie Style*, Columbia Records.

"Feels," **Pharrel Williams, Katy Perry, & Big Sean**, *Funk Wav Bounces Vol. 1*, Sony Music Entertainment.

"Things Can Only Get Better," **Howard Jones**, *Dream into Action*, Warner Music Group.

"Dancing on the Ceiling," **Lionel Richie**, *Dancing on the Ceiling*, Universal Music Group.

"Adventure of a Lifetime," **Cold Play**, *A Head Full of Dreams*, Warner Music Group.

"Virtual Insanity," **Jamiroquai**, *Traveling Without Moving*, Sony Music Entertainment.

"The Other Side," SZA, **Justin Timberlake**, *Trolls World Tour: Original Motion Picture Soundtrack*, RCA Records.

"Sweet Child O'Mine," **Guns & Roses**, *Appetite for Destruction*, Universal Music Group.

"Don't Stop Believin'," **Journey**, *Escape*, Sony Music Entertainment.

"Stayin' Alive," **Bee Gees**, *Saturday Night Fever*, RSO Records.

"Don't Stop Me Now," **Queen**, *Jazz*, Warner Music Group.

"What Lovers Do," **Maroon 5, SZA**, *Red Pill Blues*, Universal Music Group.

"Praise You," **King Arthur**, *Believe in the Kingdom*, Hexagon Record Label.

"I'm Coming Out," **Diana Ross**, *Diana*, Universal Music Group.

"Say So," **Doja Cat**, *Hot Pink*, RCA Records.

"Cheap Thrills," **Sia**, *This Is Acting*, RCA Records.

"Rapper's Delight," **The Sugarhill Gang**, *Sugarhill Gang*, Warner Music Group.

DOCK TUNES — 95

"Lovely Day," **Bill Withers**, *Menagerie*, Sony Music Entertainment.

"The Tide Is High," **Blondie**, *On the Beach*, Chrysalis Records.

"Islands in the Stream," **Dolly Parton & Kenny Rogers**, *Eyes That See in the Dark*, Sony Music Entertainment.

"Jamming," **Bob Marley & The Wailers**, *Exodus*, Universal Music Group.

"Golden Hour," **Kacey Musgraves**, *Golden Hour*, Universal Music Group.

"Say Something," **Justin Timberlake, Chris Stapleton**, *Man of the Woods*, RCA Records.

"In the Colors," **Ben Harper & The Innocent Criminals**, *Lifeline*, Universal Music Group.

"Free Fallin'," **John Mayer**, *Where the Light Is*, Universal Music Group.

"Forever in Blue Jeans," **Neil Diamond**, *You Don't Bring Me Flowers*, Sony Music Entertainment.

"Yellow Eyes," **Rayland Baxter**, *Imaginary Man*, ATO Records.

"You Are the Sunshine Of My Life," **Stevie Wonder**, *Talking Book*, Universal Music Group.

"Meant To Be," **Bebe Rexha, Florida Georgia Line**, *All Your Fault: Pt. 2*, Warner Music Group.

"From Eden," **Hozier**, *Hozier*, Rubyworks Island Columbia.

"Boa Sorte," **Vanessa Da Mata, Ben Harper,** *Sim*, Sony Music Entertainment.

"Southern Sun," **Boy & Bear**, *Harlequin Dream*, Nettwerk Music Group.

"It's Five O'Clock Somewhere," **Alan Jackson & Jimmy Buffett**, *Greatest Hits Volume II*, Sony Music Entertainment.

"Wagon Wheel," **Darius Rucker**, *True Believers*, Nettwerk Music Group.

"Dancing in the Moonlight," **Top Loader**, *Dancing in the Moonlight*, Sony Music Entertainment.

"Summer Breeze," **Jason Mraz**, *Everwood*, Nettwerk Music Group.

"These Are the Days," **Van Morrison**, *Avalon Sunset*, Universal Music Group.

"Drops of Jupiter," **Train**, *Drops of Jupiter*, Sony Music Entertainment.

SUNDAY MORNING — 160

"Home Again," **Michael Kiwanuka**, *Home Again*, Universal Music Group.

"I Say a Little Prayer," **Aretha Franklin**, *Aretha Now*, Warner Music Group.

"Tudo Muda O Tempo Toda," **Celso Fonseca**, *Angala*, O Tempo, Dudu Borges Productions.

"If the Moon Turns Green," **Billie Holiday**, *Recital*, Universal Music Group.

"Quiet Nights of Quiet Stars," **Stacey Kent**, *Dreamer in Concert*, Universal Music Group.

"Wonderful Life," **Katie Melua**, *In Winter*, Sony Music Entertainment.

"Misty Blue," **Dorothy Moore**, *Misty Blue*, Malaco Records.

"Can't Help Falling in Love," **Kina Grannis**, *The Living Room Sessions Vol. 3*, KG Records.

"September Morn," **Neil Diamond**, *September Morn*, Sony Music Entertainment.

"One Of These Things First," **Nick Drake**, *Bryter Layter*, Universal Music Group.

"Harvest Moon," **Neil Young**, *Harvest Moon*, Warner Music Group.

"Hawa Dolo," **Ali Farka Toure**, *The Source*, Warner Music Group.

"Have You Ever Seen the Rain," **Willie & Paula Nelson**, *To All the Girls. . .*, Sony Music Entertainment.

"Pretty Stars," **Bill Frisell**, *Music IS*, Okeh Records

"Feels Like Home," **Bonnie Raitt**, *Fundamental*, Universal Music Group.

"Vincent," **James Blake**, *James Blake*, A&M Records.

"My Favorite Picture of You," **Guy Clarke**, *My Favorite Picture of You*, Dualtone Records.

"Alone Again," by **Diana Krall**, *Wallflower*, Universal Music Group.

"How Can You Mend a Broken Heart," **Al Green**, *Let's Stay Together*, Universal Music Group.

"Let's Fall in Love for the Night," **Finneas**, *Blood Harmony*, Best Friends Music.

"Lesson Learned," **Alicia Keys**, *As I Am*, Sony Music Entertainment.

IN THE MOOD — 235

"Stand by My Woman," **Lenny Kravitz**, *Mama Said*, Universal Music Group.

"Can't Take My Eyes off of You," **Lauryn Hill**, *The Miseducation of Lauryn Hill*, Sony Music Entertainment.

"Wild Horses," **Alicia Keys & Adam Levine**, *Unplugged*, Sony Music Entertainment.

"Black," **Pearl Jam**, *Ten*, Sony Music Entertainment.

"Kiss from a Rose," **Seal**, *Seal*, Warner Music Group.

"Miss You," **The Rolling Stones**, *Some Girls*, Sony Music Entertainment.

"Everybody Hurts," **R.E.M.**, *Automatic for the People*, Warner Music Group.

"Love on Top," **Beyoncé**, *4*, Sony Music Entertainment.

"Wicked Game," **Chis Isaak**, *Wicked Game*, Warner Music Group.

"Something to Believe In," **Citizen Cope**, One Lovely Day, Rainwater Recordings

"All I Want Is You," **U2**, *Rattle and Hum*, Universal Music Group.

"Lost Together," **Blue Rodeo**, *Lost Together*, Warner Music Group.

"Something Just Like This," **The Chainsmokers & Coldplay**, *Memories. . .Do Not Open*, Sony Music Entertainment.

"Harvest Moon," **Neil Young**, *Harvest Moon*, Warner Music Group.

"So Far Away," **Dire Straits**, *Brothers in Arms*, Universal Music Group.

"Forever," **KISS**, *Hot In The Shade*, Universal Music Group.

"Hotel California" **Eagles**, *Hotel California*, Warner Music Group.

"Purple Rain," **Prince**, *Purple Rain*, Warner Music Group.

"Betty Davis Eyes," **Kim Carnes**, *Mistaken Identity*, EMI Records.

"Sultans of Swing," **Dire Straits**, *The Very Best of Dire Straits*, Universal Music Group.

"San San Rock," **Thievery Corporation**, *Treasures from the Temple*, Eighteenth Street Lounge Music.

MEMORIES AND MAGIC — 309

"A Case of You," **Joni Mitchell**, *Blue*, Warner Music Group.

"The Way You Look Tonight," **Frank Sinatra**, *Nothing but the Best*, Warner Music Group.

"I Could Write a Book," **Harry Connick Jr.**, *When Harry Met Sally. . .*, Sony Music Entertainment.

"Grease," **Frankie Valli**, *Grease*, RSO Records

"Hey Jude," **The Beatles**, *Hey Jude*, Apple Records.

"Wild World," **Cat Stevens**, *Tea for the Tillerman*, Universal Music Group.

"Kind & Generous," **Natalie Merchant**, *Ophelia*, Warner Music Group.

"Saturday in the Park," **Chicago**, *Chicago V*, Sony Music Entertainment.

"I Have a Dream," **ABBA**, *Voulez-Vous*, Warner Music Group.

"I'm Gonna Be (500 Miles)," **The Proclaimers**, *Sunshine on Leith*, Chrysalis Records.

"Holiday," **Madonna**, *Madonna*, Warner Music Group.

"Give a Little Bit," **Supertramp**, *Even in the Quietest Moments. . .*, Universal Music Group.

"Galileo," **Indigo Girl**s, *Rites of Passage*, Sony Music Entertainment.

"Vienna," **Billy Joel**, *The Stranger*, Sony Music Entertainment.

"Together Again," **Janet Jackson**, *The Velvet Rope*, Universal Music Group.

"Jenny from the Block," **Jennifer Lopez**, *This Is Me. . . Then*, Sony Music Entertainment.

"Don't Panic," **Cold Play**, *The Blue Room*, Warner Music Group.

"Tiny Dancer," **Elton John**, *Madman Across the Water*, Universal Music Group.

"Memories," **Maroon 5**, *Jordi*, Universal Music Group.

"I Won't Give Up," **Jason Mraz**, *Love Is a Four Letter Word*, Warner Music Group.

"Somewhere Over the Rainbow," **Israel Kamakawiwo'ole**, *Alone in IZ World*, Universal Music Group.

RESOURCES

TO THE TRADE

Arte International arte-international.com
Avenue Road avenue-road.com
Bradley USA bradleyusa.com
Bright Chair brightchair.com
Carolina Irving Textiles carolinairvingtextiles.com
Carvers' Guild carversguild.com
Chelsea Textiles chelseatextiles.com
Christopher Farr christopherfarr.com
Claremont Furnishing Fabrics Co. claremontfurnishing.com
Cole & Son Cole-and-son.com
de Gournay degournay.com
Creative Custom Furnishings creativecustomfurnishings
Fabric & Steel fabricandsteel.com
Fortuny fortuny.com
Garrison Rousseau garrisonrousseau.com
GUBI gubi.com
Hélène Aumont heleneaumont.com
Hollace Cluny hollacecluny.ca
Holland & Sherry hollandandsherry.com
Holly Hunt hollyhunt.com
Ironies ironies.com
James Duncan jamesstuartduncan.com
Janus et Cie janusetcie.com
John Robshaw johnrobshaw.com
John Rosselli & Associates johnrosselli.com
Kravet/ Lee Jofa/ Brunschwig & Fils/ GP & J Baker/ Donghia kravet.com
Les Indiennes lesindiennes.com
Lisa Fine Textiles www.lisafinetextiles.com
Made Goods madegoods.com
Mambo Factory mambofactory.pt
Memo Showroom memoshowroom.com
Merida Studio meridastudio.com
Mitchell Gold + Bob Williams mgbwhome.com
Noir noirfurniturela.com
Oly Studio olystudio.com
Opuzen opuzen.com
Palecek palecek.com
Peter Dunham Textiles peterdunhamtextiles.com
Peter Fasano Fabrics & Wallcoverings peterfasano.com
Phillip Jeffries phillipjeffries.com
Pierre Frey pierrefrey.com
Plexi-Craft plexi-craft.com
Porta Romana portaromana.com
Primavera primaverafurnishings.com
Quadrille quadrillefabrics.com
Ralph Pucci ralphpucci.com
Raoul Textiles raoultextiles.com
Robert Kime robertkime.com
Samuel & Sons samuelandsons.com
Savel Inc. savelinc.com
Sherle Wagner sherlewagner.com
Stark Carpet starkcarpet.com
The Red Carpet & Rug Company theredcarpet.ca
Theo theodecor.com
The Rug Company therugcompany.com
Threadcount threadcountinc.com
Y&Co ycocarpet.com
Scalamandré scalamandre.com

FURNISHINGS

1stDibs 1stdibs.com
CB2 cb2.ca
Crate & Barrel crateandbarrel.com
Decorum Decorative Finds ddfhome.net
Design Within Reach dwr.com
Elte & Ginger's elte.com

Jardin de Ville jardindeville.com
Jonathan Adler jonathanadler.com
Kiosk kioskdesign.ca
Knoll knoll.com
Mecox Gardens mecox.com
Mjölk www.mjolk.ca
ModShop modshop1.com
Muskoka Living shop.muskokaliving.ca
Pottery Barn potterybarn.com
Restoration Hardware restorationhardware.com
Roche Bobois roche-bobois.com
South Hill Home southhillhome.com
The Future Perfect thefutureperfect.com
Vanguard Furniture vanguardfurniture.com
Vincent Sheppard vincentsheppard.com
Walker Zabriskie Furniture walkerzabriskie.com
Waterworks waterworks.com
West Elm westelm.com

LIGHTING

Allied Maker alliedmaker.com
Ann-Morris annmorrislighting.com
Apparatus Studio apparatusstudio.com
Arteriors arteriorshome.com
Cedar & Moss cedarandmoss.com
Charles Edwards charlesedwards.com
Christopher Boots christopherboots.com
Circa Lighting circalighting.com
Coleen & Company coleenandcompany.com
Currey & Company curreyandcompany.com
Decorium decorium.com
Galerie des Lampes galeriedeslampes.com
Gabriel Scott gabriel-scott.com
Hector Finch hectorfinch.com
Hervé Van der Straeten vanderstraeten.fr
Hollis + Morris hollisandmorris.com
Hudson Valley hudsonvalleylighting.hvlgroup.com
Hinkley hinkley.com
Lightmaker Studio lightmakerstudio.com
Luminaire Authentik luminaireauthentik.com
Matthew McCormick matthewmccormick.ca
Mitzi mitzi.com
Niermann Weeks niermannweeks.com
Phoenix Day phoenixday.com
Rejuvenation rejuvenation.com
Remains Lighting remains.com
Tom Dixon tomdixon.net
The Urban Electric Co. urbanelectric.com
Vaughan Designs vaughandesigns.com
Y-Lighting ylighting.com

PAINT

Benjamin Moore benjaminmoore.com
Farrow & Ball www.farrow-ball.com

ART GALLERIES/ DEALERS

Art Interiors artinteriors.ca
Bauxi Gallery bau-xi.com
Everard Reed Gallery everard-read.co.za
Galerie de Bellefeuille debellefeuille.com
Hamburg Kennedy Art Advisory hkartadvisory.com
Kasmin Gallery kasmingallery.com
Lumas ca.lumas.com
Nicholas Metivier Gallery metiviergallery.com
Odon Wagner Gallery odonwagnergallery.com
Olga Korper Gallery Inc. olgakorpergallery.com
Samuel Owen Gallery samuelowen.com
Staley-Wise Gallery staleywise.com
Stephen Bulger Gallery bulgergallery.com

FIRST EDITION
22 23 24 25 26   5 4 3 2 1

TEXT
© 2022 Anne Hepfer
Photographic credits on page 316

PUBLISHED BY
Gibbs Smith
P.O. Box 667
Layton, Utah 84041
1.800.835.4993 orders
www.gibbs-smith.com

EDITED BY
Beth Hitchcock

PRINCIPAL PHOTOGRAPHY AND
BACK COVER PHOTO BY
Virginia Macdonald

DESIGNED BY
Rose Pereira

Printed and bound in China
Gibbs Smith books are printed on either recycled, 100% post-consumer waste, FSC-certified papers
or on paper produced from sustainable PEFC-certified forest/controlled wood source.
Learn more at www.pefc.org.

Library of Congress Control Number: 2022930974

ISBN 978-1423661511